...ry Christmas
to Carolyn
Love Mom '96

...ry Christmas
to Carolyn
Love Mom '96

ROYAL
SCANDALS

ROYAL SCANDALS

DIANE OSEN

MetroBooks

MetroBooks

AN IMPRINT OF FRIEDMAN/FAIRFAX, PUBLISHERS

Library of Congress Cataloging-in-Publication Data

Osen, Diane, 1956-
    Royal Scandals: true tales of sex, lust, and greed / Diane Osen
        p.   cm.
    Includes bibliographal references (p.) and index.
    ISBN 1-56799-161-0 (hc)
    ISBN 1-56799-203-X (pb)
    1. Kings and rulers--Conduct of life--History. 2. Heads of state-
-Conduct of life--History. 3. Scandals. I. Title.
    D107.S78   1995
    920.02--dc20
    [B]   94-34641
                                         CIP

Editor: Susan Lauzau
Art Director: Jeff Batzli
Designer: Andrea Karman
Photography Editor: Jennifer Crowe McMichael

Color seperations by Sele & Color
Printed in Italy

For bulk purchases and special sales, please contact:
Friedman/Fairfax Publishers
Attention: Sales Department
15 West 26th Street
New York, NY 10010
212/685-6610 FAX 212/685-1307

✂ —— Dedication —— ✄

To Rick and Serena Covkin,
my ruling passions

Acknowledgments

Sincere thanks to Gary Jurczynski, for his technical assistance; to my family and friends, for their boundless kindness; and to the many writers whose research and insights made this book possible.

Contents

INTRODUCTION

For as long as history has been recorded, people around the world have been fascinated by royalty. No matter where or when or how well they have reigned, kings and queens and emperors and czars have always been able to command our attention, because they alone embody our most **thrilling fantasies** of absolute power, and our most nagging fears of inevitable decline. Masters of all they survey, they are nonetheless as vulnerable to unruly desires as any of their subjects—but unlike the rest of us, when they give in to their ruling passions, their actions can alter the course of history.

Royal Scandals: True Tales of Sex, Lust, and Greed recounts some of the most **shocking,** sordid, touching, and incredible episodes in royal history. From the brutal dynasties of ancient Asia to the bitterly divided empires of the Renaissance and the Enlightenment to the badly demoralized monarchies of Western Europe today, *Royal Scandals* explores the obsessive desires for love, **sex,** excess, power, and revenge that shaped the lives—and rocked the empires—of the world's most celebrated royal families.

In researching *Royal Scandals*, what struck me most was the dichotomy between the fabulous pageantry of public life and the ordinary problems of private life that plagued rulers throughout history. Russia's Ivan the Terrible typified this enduring duality: like so many other sovereigns, he enjoyed a court that was incredibly lavish, yet despite his immense wealth and **power,** he was unable to defend himself against the personal demons that blighted his life.

Although he is best known today for the many atrocities he committed during his reign, Ivan was in many ways a highly cerebral and forward-thinking czar: blessed with considerable literary skills, his other talents included an ear for music and a prodigious memory. His appreciation for goldsmithing and keen interest in history inspired a renaissance in these areas.

The czar's hospitality, too, was renowned. His regular banquets for thousands of guests began with Ivan greeting each guest by name and presenting him with a piece of bread; immediately thereafter several hundred roasted swans were carved into morsels, and presented to each nobleman with the words, "The czar gives you this." Subsequent courses—including delicacies such as roasted peacocks adorned with their feathers, stuffed storks, and **gilded** trees from which cakes and sweetmeats had been suspended—were served in jewel-encrusted vessels, fashioned in the shape of animals, that were so heavy a dozen men were required to carry just one.

Princess Grace and Prince Rainier dance at a costume ball.

Yet in his **private** life, Ivan often acted more like a monster than a sovereign. Subject from childhood to overwhelming attacks of rage, he tortured, imprisoned, or executed scores of his political supporters after the death of his first wife, and indulged in innumerable **orgies.** Afterward, he wounded himself in acts of contrition, and then went on to commit further atrocities. It was in just such a state of rage that Ivan murdered his own son, after the young man defended his wife, whose dress Ivan had criticized. Overwhelmed by sorrow, the czar became a recluse and an insomniac, bursting into uncontrollable tears and laughter, and wandering from one church to another, wailing. He died, just as sixty **witches** had predicted he would, while playing chess with Boris Gudonov in 1584.

History reveals that Ivan's story was not unique; nearly every sovereign who left behind an indelible imprint experienced that same tug-of-war between his or her ruling passions and the passion to rule. In some cases, these conflicts led to scandals so outrageous they rocked empires; think of Henry VIII of England executing his wives and fomenting decades of murderous religious strife in order to justify his penchant for **adultery.** Happily, other monarchs have been more successful in satisfying—or hiding—their scandalous obsessions, a skill that has enabled the monarchy to flourish into the twentieth century, when few believe any longer that kingship is a divine right.

But even if history has proven that kings and queens and emperors and czars are as imperfect as the rest of us, there remains an overwhelming desire to believe in their perfection. Having been unable to rid our lives of all the age-old horrors and disappointments—war, famine, illness, **divorce** — we remain obsessed with these figures from a fairy tale, whose fabulous wealth and unlimited power still seem to offer the last best chance for a better world. *Royal Scandals* is testimony to that obsession, and to the ruling passions of the sovereigns who have always inspired it.

Unable to rid our lives of age-old *horrors,* we remain obsessed with these figures from a fairy tale.

Edward VIII, the eleven-month king, in his coronation robes.

CHAPTER ONE

You Can't Always

Get What You Want

✤ Royal ✤

Weddings

Grace Kelly marries Prince Rainier *(left)*; the marriage of Queen Victoria and Prince Albert *(above)*

ost of us choose to marry people we love. But love has almost never inspired the proposals of royals, nor has it ensured their fidelity. ⚜ Their marriages have most often been speculative ventures, undertaken in the hope of cementing political alliances, enhancing their nations' prestige, or producing legitimate heirs. More often than not, it is their lovers who have been rewarded with their affection and trust. ⚜

Nonetheless, marriage is of great significance to royalty today, for it has come to fulfill another important purpose: that of saving an obsolete institution from sure extinction. Having lost their political and moral authority, royalty on the brink of the twenty-first century reign only in the realm of the imagination. ⚜ Luckily for them, nothing indulges our fantasies like the wedding of two gorgeous young royals. ⚜ Watching as these figures from a fairy tale take their vows, even the most cynical among us find ourselves believing that dreams really can come true. ⚜

Love Among the Ancients

In ancient times, romance—whether real or imagined by the masses—rarely played a role in royal weddings. Cheops, the Egyptian pharoah who built the Great Pyramid of Gizeh some five thousand years ago, was forced by custom to marry some of his sisters and half-sisters, as well as one of his stepmothers—a tradition much more likely to inspire murder than lust. Happily, the customs of the age also required the pharoah to maintain an enormous harem of concubines.

Alexander the Great Lover

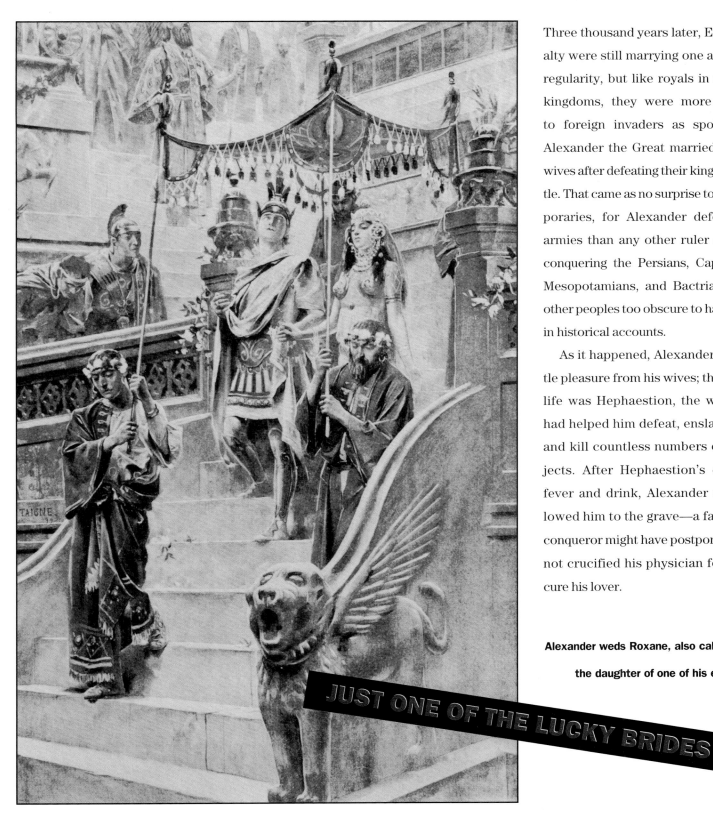

Three thousand years later, Egyptian royalty were still marrying one another with regularity, but like royals in many other kingdoms, they were more often wed to foreign invaders as spoils of war. Alexander the Great married two of his wives after defeating their kingdoms in battle. That came as no surprise to his contemporaries, for Alexander defeated more armies than any other ruler of his time, conquering the Persians, Cappadocians, Mesopotamians, and Bactrians—among other peoples too obscure to have survived in historical accounts.

As it happened, Alexander derived little pleasure from his wives; the love of his life was Hephaestion, the warrior who had helped him defeat, enslave, torture, and kill countless numbers of new subjects. After Hephaestion's death from fever and drink, Alexander quickly followed him to the grave—a fate the great conqueror might have postponed if he had not crucified his physician for failing to cure his lover.

Alexander weds Roxane, also called Rushanak, the daughter of one of his enemies.

JUST ONE OF THE LUCKY BRIDES

✠

Hilda was widowed after one night, Attila having finally *succumbed* to the demands of the marriage bed.

✠

Playboy of the Western World

Like Alexander, Attila the Hun was a one-man crime wave with little interest in the niceties of courtship. Born in 395, he had a typical Hun childhood: his face was scarred and his nose flattened with boards and bandages while he was still an infant, and he grew up watching his people subdue one European kingdom after another. The Huns' reputation for pillage and murder was so widespread that by the time Attila came to power in 433, his main source of income came from Theodosius, the Emperor of the East, who thought no sum too great to pay if it prevented the Huns from invading his territories. Later, Valentian III, the Emperor of the West, was forced to pay off Attila as well, and, delighted by this new tribute, the Hun king decided to marry again—for the 301st time. His bride was Hilda, a beautiful young blonde whose parents he had murdered in his campaign against Valentian. She was widowed after their first night together, Attila having finally succumbed to the demands of the marital bed.

Love, Renaissance Style

Given the almost constant warfare during the Renaissance among the tiny states that today constitute Italy, it is no wonder that their rulers elevated matchmaking to an art form, on par with those other notorious practices of the period, Machiavellian politics and poisoning.

Ercole d'Este, the most famous duke of fifteenth-century Ferrara, was undoubtedly the preeminent royal matchmaker of his day, an exceedingly shrewd and ambitious patriarch who valued political expediency above all else—including the lives of his children. His most notorious achievement was the marriage of his son and heir Alfonso to the legendary Lucrezia Borgia. A striking woman, she had bright yellow hair that she washed weekly with a concoction of saffron, box shavings, wood ash, barley straw, madder, and cumin seed. Of course, it was not for her hair alone that Lucrezia was famous; her reputation sprang from her family's penchant for assassination, preferably by poison. Her older brother Cesare was especially adept at murder, and it is believed that he killed Lucrezia's second husband, the timid seventeen-year-old Alfonso of Aragon.

After Alfonso of Aragon's death, Ercole d'Este began negotiating for Lucrezia's betrothal to his own son Alfonso, whose first marriage, at the age of fifteen, had ended with the death in childbirth of his equally youthful wife. Although Alfonso balked at first, he warmed to the idea after his father managed to secure a dowry estimated at the equivalent of three million dollars, as well as two castles in Bologna and a reduction in the Ferrara's annual tribute to the papacy. The couple was married by proxy on December 30, 1501, after which Lucrezia made the long journey to Ferrara, where she was crowned duchess four years later. Despite its inauspicious beginnings, their seventeen-year marriage was considered something of a success, for neither killed the other.

Lucrezia Borgia's sinister reputation was largely due to the political machinations of her father, Pope Alexander VI, and her brother, Cesare, depicted here in a painting by Dante Gabriel Rosetti. Her two betrothals and three marriages, all by the age of twenty-two, helped mold her image as a treacherous mate, and the murders of one of her husbands and several of her lovers solidified it.

Queen Mary the Innocent

In Renaissance England, Queen Mary also felt obliged to marry for political reasons. A thirty-seven-year-old virgin when she ascended the throne in 1553, she was so inexperienced in sexual matters that she had never so much as heard the word "whore"; when she heard it for the first time, she repeated it to her lady-in-waiting as a term of endearment. A fervent Catholic, she typically wore a religious habit under her magnificent gowns and was opposed to marrying anyone but a royal who shared her religious faith.

Five months after Mary was crowned, she announced that she had decided to marry her cousin Philip of Spain, the heir of the Holy Roman Emperor. Throughout England, Mary's Protestant subjects complained bitterly about her choice, with the opposition even attempting a coup. But Mary held firm to her choice, despite her reservations about returning the amorous advances of a husband ten years younger than she, and in his sexual prime. Nonetheless, according to the emperor's envoy to England, she promised that if she did marry Philip she would fall very deeply in love with him, but only because the Church commanded a wife to love her husband. Mary knew that however much the idea of sex disgusted her, it was her duty to submit. The couple was wed in Winchester Cathedral on July 25, 1554.

Just a few months later, Mary's anxiety about sex was replaced by a delusion that she had conceived a child with her new and singularly inattentive husband. In fact, she had been stricken with dropsy, which causes various parts of the

DESPERATELY SEEKING AN HEIR

Philip and Mary were never able to produce a child.

body to swell. Philip remained in England only long enough to determine the truth, and did not return to his wife's side until the following year. Once again Mary hoped that she might be pregnant—and was once again crushed to learn that she had been mistaken. Five years after her coronation, beset by political problems, utterly dispirited by her unhappy mar-

riage, and devastated by her failure to bear a child who would continue the succession, she died alone in her bed after several days of delirious dreams about children. Two weeks later, in a letter to his sister, Philip wrote, "the Queen my wife is dead. May God have received her into His Glory. I felt a reasonable regret for her death."

The Harems of Russia

Although unhappy marriages were also common among Russian royalty, politics did not play the same important role in royal matchmaking; isolated from much of Europe and devoted to their own religious traditions, the imperial family concentrated instead on producing legitimate heirs.

During the seventeenth and eighteenth centuries, the czars simply sent couriers across the country to seek out and bring back to Moscow—by force, if necessary—the most eligible girls of marriageable age. Vasily Ivanovich, for example, who was the father of Ivan the Terrible, chose his bride from among fifteen hundred such girls; his son chose from among two thousand. The girls were housed in a special dormitory, where they slept twelve to a room throughout the selection process. Every day, the prospective bridegroom would visit this harem and observe each girl individually, throwing down a handkerchief studded with pearls to signal her dismissal. When at last a future czarina was selected, she was expected not only to submit, but to turn over to her new husband her sisters and other close female relatives.

Ivan and his czarina, Anastasia, the first of his seven wives, were wed in a traditional Russian Orthodox ceremony, standing together on a red damask cloth fringed with sable; they spent their honeymoon at a monastery, where they went to Lent services daily for a week. From then on, Anastasia was rarely seen in public, having been secured in special all-female quarters known as the terem. Dressed in elaborate headdresses and long veils, she spent her days there in prayer.

Ivan's wives led precarious lives; he divorced two and arranged for the murder of another. Three more were poisoned, apparently the victims of Ivan's enemies. His seventh wife survived him.

Ivan, who married mainly to produce heirs, killed his eldest son, leaving two less-suitable heirs.

State-sanctioned Voyeurism

At Versailles, during the reign of Louis XIV, every aspect of the king's life became an opportunity for his exultation and glorification. Even Louis's rising in the morning and retiring at night were ritualized in the ceremonies of *lever* and *coucher*. Royal meals, too, were public performances, and it was considered a great honor to watch the king eat. Each courtier had to wear a hat and was required to remove it whenever he spoke to or was addressed by the king.

Moreover, it was the king's right to participate, albeit vicariously, in even the most intimate of his family's marriage rituals. For example, after Louis's fifteen-year-old grandson, the duc de Bourgogne, was wed to twelve-year-old Marie Adelaide of Savoy, the king accompanied the bridal couple to their bedchamber to certify that the newlyweds had indeed been in bed together; he forbade them, however, to have sex for another two years. When the ban had passed, Louis promised to come again to their quarters at Versailles to see them engage in their first act of love, but, fortunately for them, he arrived too late to have that pleasure.

The king promised to come to *see* them engage in their first act of love.

One of the Few True Royal Love Stories

✠

"He clasped me in his arms, and we *kissed* each other again and again."

✠

Dear Diary

Passages from Victoria's diary show her devotion to Albert:

1-4 November, 1839: He was so affectionate, so kind, so dear, we kissed each other again and again and he called me 'Liebe Kleine. Ich habe dich so lieb, ich kann nicht sagen wie.' [Darling little one. I love you so much, I can't express how much.]...Oh! what too sweet delightful moments are these!!...We sit so nicely side by side on that little blue sofa; no two Lovers could ever be happier than we are!...He took my hands in his, and said my hands were so little he could hardly believe they were hands, as he had hitherto only been accustomed to handle hands like Ernest's.

12 February, 1840: Already the 2nd. day since our marriage...I feel a purer more unearthly feeling than I ever did...We sat in my large sitting room; he at one table, I at another, and we both tried to write, I my journal, and Albert a letter, but it ended always in talking.

13 February, 1840: Got up at 20 m. to 9. My dearest Albert put on my stockings for me. I went in and saw him shave; a great delight to me.

Prince Albert had such an influence on Victoria that some called her "Queen Albertine."

Whatever the customs of their nations, relatively few royal spouses seem to have truly loved each another. For female monarchs in particular, happiness in marriage almost always remained elusive—with the famous exception of that most famously exceptional queen, Victoria of England.

There was nothing in Victoria's background to suggest that she would succeed in marriage where so many of her fore-bears had miserably failed. Her father, the duke of Kent, had married only to secure financial aid from Parliament, discarding in the process his mistress of thirty years, a prostitute named Julie St. Laurent. One of Victoria's uncles, King William IV, whom she succeeded, had likewise married a princess after abandoning his longtime mistress, the beautiful actress Dorothy Jordan, and the ten illegitimate children they had produced together. Another uncle, the duke of Cumberland, was a well-known sexual deviant with a taste for incest who had married a woman widely believed to have murdered both of her spouses.

Yet Victoria seems never to have doubted her own prospects for a happy marriage. She fell in love at first sight with her future consort and first cousin, Prince Albert of Saxe-Coburg, noting in her diary on October 10, 1839, that it "was with some emotion that I beheld Albert—who is so beautiful." The next day she wrote, "Albert really is quite charming, and so excessively handsome, such beautiful blue eyes, an exquisite nose, and such a pretty mouth with delicate moustachios and slight but very slight whiskers; a beautiful figure, broad in the shoulders and a fine waist." By

October 15, she was so overcome by passion that she broke protocol and proposed to him herself, saying "that I thought he must be aware...that it would make me too happy if he would consent to what I wished (to marry me). We embraced each other and he was so kind, so affectionate...that I really felt it was the happiest, brightest moment of my life." Their marriage was set for February 10, 1840, in Royal Chapel, St. James.

Victoria defied convention again during her wedding ceremony by promising rapturously to obey her new husband as part of her vows; because her husband would be one of her subjects, it was not usual for a queen to pledge obedience to her husband. But like all royal brides of the time, she wore white for the occasion, a tradition inaugurated in 1499 by Anne of Brittany when she married King

Louis XII of France. Her satin gown, however, was probably not originally intended as a wedding dress at all; certainly, the delicate Honiton lace that graced its neckline had been commissioned long before her engagement to help employ two hundred impoverished lace makers in Devon.

After the ceremony, she and Albert had only thirty minutes alone together, on a sofa in Buckingham Palace, before they joined their guests at an enormous wedding breakfast. They then set out on a four-day honeymoon at Windsor, remarkable to the young queen for the "feelings of heavenly love and happiness...I never could have hoped to have felt before! He clasped me in his arms, and we kissed each other again and again!...Oh! This was the happiest day of my life!"

Nicholas and Alexandra

Some of Victoria's grandchildren also enjoyed happy unions with their spouses, most notably her favorite granddaughter, Princess Alix of Hesse, who took the title Empress Alexandra after she married Nicholas, the last of the Russian czars.

Tall, blue-eyed, and crowned with a mane of golden-red hair, Alix was raised by her mother, the former Princess of Wales, and her father, Grand Duke Louis of Hesse, in a palace in Darmstadt that might just as easily have graced the English countryside: decorated with pictures and mementos of the princess's native England, it even housed an English nanny, who served the royal offspring English treats like rice pudding and baked apples. However, Alix had more opportu-

HOPELESSLY DEVOTED

Passionately in love with his wife and unwilling to oppose her wishes, Nicholas once signed a letter to Alexandra, "Your poor little weak-willed hubby."

Nicholas and Alexandra had four daughters and a son, Alexei, who suffered from hemophilia. While Alexandra staunchly believed that her husband had a divine mission to rule Russia, Nicholas himself would likely have preferred a quiet life with his family.

nities than she wished to savor the pleasures of English life; after her mother and sister died of diphtheria, she began spending a great deal of time with her grandmother, the Queen of England, at Windsor, Balmoral, and Osborne.

Alix was twelve years old when she first met Nicholas in St. Petersburg, at the wedding of her sister Elisabeth to Grand Duke Sergei. Nicholas was also related to the British royal family: his aunt was Princess Alexandra, the wife of the future King Edward VII. Nicholas enjoyed his visits with the royal family and delighted in his famously dapper

uncle's generosity at the establishments of assorted tailors, bootmakers, and hatters. Dressed in the height of fashion, Nicholas resembled his first cousin, the future George V.

When Nicholas met Alix for the second time, in 1889, she had blossomed into a beautiful seventeen-year-old, and he eagerly accompanied her on a round of balls and other parties; after she left Russia, he realized that he had fallen irrevocably in love. His parents, on the other hand, were not nearly as entranced by Alix; they had hoped that he would make a more substantial match, and were

apparently aware that the princess from Hesse had already turned down a proposal from Prince Albert Edward of England, a grandson of Victoria and the heir presumptive to the British throne.

Instead of being distressed, Queen Victoria was impressed by Alix's resolve in declining to be Eddy's wife. She wrote, "This shows great strength of character as all her family and all of us wish it, and she refused the greatest position there is." Nicholas was also pleased by her decision, though for very different reasons. In 1892 he wrote in his diary, "My dream is some day to marry Alix H. I have loved her a long while and still deeper and stronger since 1889 when she spent six weeks in St. Petersburg."

By 1894, Nicholas's parents had relented in their opposition to a match with Alix, and told their son that he could propose to the princess that spring, when the entire royal family was to gather at Coburg for the wedding of Alix's older brother. The only obstacle now standing in his way was Alix herself, who liked Nicholas well enough, but abhorred the notion of renouncing Lutheranism and converting to the Russian Orthodox faith—a conversion required of every new member of the imperial family. After Nicholas proposed, he recalled, "she cried the whole time and only whispered now and then, 'No, I cannot.'"

With that, the future czar turned to his powerful relatives for help: first Victoria, and then Kaiser Wilhelm spoke to the princess, explaining that Lutheranism and Russian Orthodoxy were not so very different. After their encouragement failed to change her mind, Alix's sister Elisabeth importuned her to accept Nicholas's proposal, and the following day, Nicholas wrote, "We were left alone and with her first words she consented. I cried like a child, and she did too, but her expression had changed. Her face was lit by a quiet contentment."

That summer, the newly engaged couple spent six weeks with Victoria in England, where Nicholas presented his future wife with his engagement gifts: a pink pearl ring and a matching pink pearl necklace; a chain bracelet with an enormous emerald; and a sapphire and diamond brooch. The future czar had also brought along a gift from his ailing father: a sautoir of pearls, fashioned by Fabergé,

worth some 250,000 rubles. During this same visit, Nicholas and Alix were named godparents to his cousin George's son David, the future King Edward VIII, and Alix began leaving loving messages in Nicholas's ever present diary.

But their idyll was shattered by the death of Nicholas's father of acute nephritis just ten days after he had struggled out of his sickbed to welcome his future daughter-in-law back to Russia. Nicholas, now czar, led the mourning as his father's funeral procession wended its way from Moscow to St. Petersburg, where the royal family had gathered once again. For seventeen days, the body of the deceased czar lay exposed in his casket in the Fortress of Saint Peter and Paul; and it was in this atmosphere that Alix, now Alexandra Feodorovna, and Nicholas were wed in a Russian Orthodox ceremony.

Despite the air of sorrow over the death of Czar Alexander that permeated the event, the wedding was counted a great success by the many royal relatives in attendance. The future George V of England wrote, in a letter to his wife, Mary, that Alix "looked too wonderfully lovely. I think Nicky is a lucky man…and I must say I never saw two people more in love." Alexandra's thoughts, on the other hand, revolved around her own good luck; on her wedding night she wrote in her husband's diary, "At last united, bound for life, and when this life is ended, we meet again in the other world and remain together for eternity." The following morning, she added this postscript: "Never did I believe there could be such utter happiness in this world, such a feeling of unity between two mortal beings. I love you, these three words have my life in them."

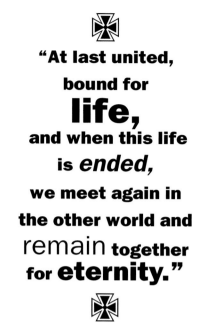

"At last united, bound for life, and when this life is *ended*, we meet again in the other world and remain together for eternity."

Kissing Cousins

By the twentieth century, more and more of Victoria's descendants, as well as their counterparts in other realms, were marrying for love rather than political expediency. This sea change in royal matrimonial options coincided—fortuitously—with two other significant changes: the waning influence of monarchs around the world and the growing importance of the mass media. Alarmed by the implications of their increasing irrelevance, royalty realized that the only way to save their cherished way of life was to expose it, albeit carefully, to the mass audiences of radio and television. By allowing ordinary citizens to participate vicariously in the rites and rituals of royalty, monarchs hoped to regain and retain the public's fascination with them; and what could be more fascinating, or better suited to a media blitz, than a royal wedding?

The first royal wedding broadcast for mass consumption was that of England's Princess Elizabeth and Philip Mountbatten (né Schleswig-Holstein-Sonderburg-Glucksburg), on November 20, 1947. According to her governess, Elizabeth fell in love with her handsome cousin on the day they met. She was then the shy, serious, thirteen-year-old heir to the British crown; he was the dashing eighteen-year-old heir to the throne of Greece. But while she was raised in a style befitting a princess, his childhood was almost Dickensian.

Elizabeth was born in 1926, the elder daughter of the future King George VI and Queen Elizabeth. After a childhood marred by an unstable nanny and distant parents, George was determined to create an entirely different kind of home life for Elizabeth and her younger sister Margaret—one filled with games, laughter, dogs, and a great deal of love. Indeed, home was where the little princesses spent so much of their time that they were acquainted with very few people outside the royal family until they were practically adults. Elizabeth's introduction to the wider world came at the end of World War II, when she joined the women's branch of the army and became the only British royal in history to qualify as a motor mechanic.

The young Princess Elizabeth poses in her wedding gown with her new husband—and cousin—Prince Philip of Greece, after their marriage in Westminster Abbey by the Archbishop of Canterbury.

Princess Elizabeth endeared herself to the British public by training as a driver in the Auxiliary Territorial Service during World War II. Here, at age nineteen, she practices taking out the plugs of a car at an ATS training center in southern England.

The **king** agreed to the *marriage* after satisfying himself that their close **blood ties** would be unlikely to affect the health of their future **children.**

Philip's youth, on the other hand, was considerably more peripatetic. A great-grandson of Queen Victoria and a nephew of Lord Mountbatten, he was the fifth child of Prince Andrew of Denmark and Greece and Princess Alice of Battenberg—royals so impoverished, says one biographer, that Princess Alice was forced to give birth to her son on a dining room table in a cottage that had neither heat nor hot water. He and his siblings were raised in exile, after their father was banished from Greece for his role in an unsuccessful military campaign against the Turks. Philip's prospects for the future

seemed dim until 1935, when the young prince was taken in hand by his uncle Lord Mountbatten and transferred from a well-known German secondary school to Gordonstoun, a sister institution located in Scotland. Afterward, Philip attended Dartmouth Naval College and then distinguished himself as a lieutenant in the Royal Navy during World War II—all the while pursuing Elizabeth.

Even after several years' acquaintance, says a biographer of George V, the royal family still felt so uncomfortable with Philip that they could not react joyfully to the news that Elizabeth

Elizabeth was not just a *breathtaking* bride but a dazzling embodiment of everything the British monarchy had been and would be again.

wished to be his wife; they thought he was rough, ill-mannered, uneducated, and would probably not be faithful. Moreover, the king seemed unwilling to accept the fact that his daughter was old enough for romance, much less marriage. Nonetheless, he finally agreed to the marriage after satisfying himself that her close blood ties to Philip would be unlikely to affect the health of their future children.

Philip promptly became a naturalized British citizen and renounced his claim to the Greek throne—and then anglicized his name to Mountbatten to obscure his German lineage. Princess Elizabeth's family had only recently changed its own name to Windsor for that very reason, but so concerned was Buckingham Palace about its future sovereign's in-laws that none of Philip's four sisters was allowed to attend the wedding. All had married German princes or dukes, and one of his brothers-in-law, Prince Cristoph von Hesse, has reportedly been suspected of providing the Nazis with the detailed knowledge they needed to bomb London during the war.

Needless to say, the absence of Philip's sisters was not among the facts reported widely by the media covering the wedding. They focused instead on promoting Elizabeth and her consort as figures out of a fairy tale—a fantasy the British public was only too eager to embrace after all the deprivations of World War II. Even the royal family seemed desperate for relief after six years of austerity; according to Lady Airlie, lady-in-waiting to Elizabeth's mother, "Most of us were sadly shabby—anyone fortunate enough to have a new dress drew all eyes—but all the famous diamonds came out again, even

though most of them had not been cleaned since 1939."

Of course, the most dazzling array of jewels was worn by the bride, who had never looked more radiant than she did walking down the long aisle of Westminster Abbey on November 20, 1947. Dressed in a spectacular Norman Hartnell gown studded with ten thousand pearls and crowned with a diamond tiara, Elizabeth was not just a breathtaking bride, but a dazzling embodiment of everything the British monarchy had been and would be again. Befitting a future queen, her wedding gifts included a cache of precious jewels from Burma, British Columbia, and South Africa; a diamond tiara that had once belonged to Queen Victoria; and earrings featuring antique pearls and a collection of every cut of diamond, which had been among Queen Anne's most cherished treasures. Philip was also showered with gifts, but the one he prized most came from his new father-in-law, who conferred on him the title of duke of Edinburgh.

Despite the magnificence of her dress and the splendor of her marriage rites, Elizabeth was perceived by her subjects as a princess with a common touch—so much so that her honeymoon at Lord Mountbatten's estate had to be cut short after hordes of reporters and sightseers camped outside the walls, hoping to catch a glimpse of the newlyweds. Elizabeth's popularity was assured and the symbolic importance of the monarch was reasserted. The royal family's romancing of the media, which had commenced with the unanticipated coronation of Elizabeth's father and intensified with the passage of World War II, had paid off handsomely.

Following their church wedding in Monaco, Princess Grace and Prince Rainier wave from a window of the royal palace.

The Monarch and the Movie Star

But for all the excitement generated by Princess Elizabeth's nuptials, it was the marriage of His Serene Highness Rainier III of Monaco to Academy Award winner Grace Kelly that established the symbiotic relationship between royalty and the media that endures to this day.

Even their introduction—engineered by MGM at the 1955 Cannes Film Festival—was an exercise in promotion. It began inauspiciously, when an electrical blackout at her hotel forced Grace to wear to their meeting the only ensemble in her closet that didn't require ironing: a highly

inappropriate black satin evening dress, festooned with enormous red roses, and a makeshift hat. Worse, she and the prince spent far more time admiring the exotic animals housed in his private zoo than they did in private conversation; yet both of them were to confide later that their mutual attraction had been instantaneous. According to Grace's biographer, that very evening Rainier declared to his spiritual adviser, "I've met her. I've met the one." For her part, Grace said later, "I almost knew I was in love with the prince before we met for the second time."

Their meeting couldn't have come at a better time for Grace. After a series of disillusioning affairs with older leading men, including Bing Crosby and William Holden, she was ready to become a wife and mother—the only roles, she had been taught to believe, that truly represented achievement for a woman. But according to her one-time lover and lifelong friend Don Richardson, Grace also hoped that marriage would help her achieve an even greater prize: the love of a father who had always preferred his other children. Richardson told a

Princess Stephanie with baby Louis.

The Grimaldis of Monaco

It took only a moment for the brown Rover to spin out of control over the last dangerous curve of the Moyenne Corniche before crashing into a hillside overlooking a cemetery. It was 10:05 a.m. on September 13, 1982, and at that instant the royal family of Monaco suffered a loss from which they have yet to recover; for by the time her daughter Stephanie was able to climb out of the driver's side of the car to call for help, Princess Grace was already in a coma that would prove fatal.

The morning of the accident, says biographer Robert Lacy, Grace and Stephanie had clashed over Stephanie's relationship with Paul Belmondo, the son of actor Jean-Paul Belmondo. While driving, Grace suffered a slight stroke, one that would have caused little damage under other circumstances. But on the CD 27 any lapse in concentration is swiftly punished, and by the time Grace's car came to a stop she had suffered head injuries too severe to be reversed.

At the time of the crash, Grace's first-born, Princess Caroline, was a ravishing young divorcée who had come of age on the front pages of Europe's tabloids. In 1983 she married a second time, taking as her husband Stephano Casiraghi, the son of an Italian industrialist. He too died tragically, in a 1990 speedboat accident, leaving Caroline with three small children. Although she has radically recast her public persona in her mother's image, it remains unclear whether good works will be enough to fill the void that death has left in her life.

Prince Albert has rarely made headlines, despite the fact that he has been linked with beauties like Brooke Shields and Claudia Schiffer. Indeed, the most pressing question surrounding the prince is whether he will ever marry; having reportedly denied rumors that he is homosexual, he maintains the lowest profile of all of Grace's children while he waits to take the reins of power.

Princess Stephanie assumed with a vengeance the role of royalty's enfant terrible that her sister had finally relinquished. A would-be actress/rock star/dress designer, she is most famous today for being the first princess in Monaco's history to have given birth out of wedlock.

biographer that "the thing she wanted most in the world was to win [her father's] approval, to make him think highly of her. And, despite everything she had accomplished, she still hadn't been able to achieve that....His son's rowing medals were far more important to him than Grace's acting awards....As far as I'm concerned, the real reason that she married the Prince was to make a bigger splash than a pair of oars."

Rainier, for years one of the world's most eligible bachelors, was also more than ready to take a spouse. His long affair with a French actress had ended with the discovery that she would be unable to bear him children—a disaster to be averted at all costs, since without an heir Rainier would eventually be obliged by law to oversee the absorption of Monaco into the Republic of France. He, too, had suffered at the hands of an unloving parent—in his case, his mother—and was no doubt thrilled by the prospect of marrying an incomparable beauty who not only shared his devotion to the Catholic Church, but whose very presence in his tiny country would immeasurably aid its economy.

After a fertility test, and Mr. Kelly's agreement to provide Rainier with a two-million-dollar dowry, Grace and Prince Rainier announced their engagement at a press conference at her parents' home in Philadelphia. The race was now on to plan, and publicize, the world's most sensational royal nuptials to date, set for April 19, 1956, in Monaco.

More than fifteen hundred journalists and untold numbers of tourists jammed the narrow streets of the world's smallest country in the days before the ceremony. A documentary film crew, dispatched by

Grace's studio, MGM, was also on hand to record the proceedings, seen live on television by some thirty million people in nine countries. The couple was actually married twice—once in a private civil ceremony conducted in the Throne Room of the palace that was to be Grace's new home and then again in a religious ceremony the following day at the Cathedral of Saint Nicholas.

Nearly seven hundred guests were on hand for the wedding mass, whose solemnity was leavened considerably both by the terrible overcrowding of the cathedral and by the heart-stopping beauty of the bride. No expense had been spared on her wedding gown, which had been designed by MGM's Helen Rose and shipped to Monaco in a steel case. It was a confection of 125-year-old rose-point lace lavished with one hundred yards of silk net, twenty-five yards of silk taffeta, and a beribboned tulle train four feet long. Beneath her dress, Grace wore three petticoats embroidered with tiny blue bows, and on her head was a veil strewn with thousands of tiny seed pearls that shimmered in the lights of the television cameras.

After the ceremony, Grace and Rainier rode in an open Rolls-Royce to the shrine of Saint Devote, patroness of Monaco, where Grace prayed; then she and her new husband joined their guests at the palace for a luncheon of lobster and champagne before embarking on a seven-week honeymoon on board the yacht *Deo Juvante II*. The prince and princess both acknowledged later that they began their first voyage as husband and wife in a virtual state of shock over the media blitz occasioned by their wedding—despite their own complicity in the process.

Addicted

to Love

❧ Royal ❧

Mark Antony with his beloved Cleopatra (left); Prince Charles and Camilla Parker Bowles (above)

ince the beginning of royal history, monarchs have pursued their passion for sex as enthusiastically as their passion for power, possessions, and preeminence. ✤ In ancient times, when sovereigns ruled absolutely, no one who treasured life dared defy their desires, even if it meant turning over one's wife or oneself for royal delectation. ✤ More recently, kings and queens and emperors and czars have satisfied their appetites for sex outside marriage with far less cruelty but just as much heat; for them, lust is not a temptation to be overcome, but a craving to be satisfied as quickly as possible. ✤ Indeed, throughout history very few monarchs have failed to treat themselves to the partners they wished to possess. ✤ Through the ages, heads of state have kept strings of lovers, either willing or coerced, sometimes disposing of them in deadly ways. ✤

Antony and Cleopatra—and Caesar

In 51 B.C. Julius Caesar jeopardized both his marriage and his authority out of an overwhelming desire to possess Cleopatra. Legend has it that the aging emperor first made the acquaintance of the nineteen-year-old queen when she unexpectedly stepped out of a magnificent Oriental carpet that had been presented to him as a gift. Having succeeded in gaining his attention, Cleopatra then appealed to Caesar to intervene in her longstanding feud with Ptolemy XIV, who was not only her co-regent, but also her brother and husband.

Although Caesar managed to reconcile the two, Egypt was nonetheless plunged into a bitter civil war. Siding with Cleopatra in defense of the city of Alexandria, Caesar nearly lost his life but eventually managed to restore her to the throne. However, instead of returning home to govern, he refused to leave the beguiling queen, waiting to return to Rome until she had given birth to their son Caesarion—a decision that angered both his supporters and detractors. Eighteen months later Cleopatra traveled to Rome to visit Caesar, but their idyll ended after only four days, when Caesar was assassinated in the senate by conspirators who feared his lust for power. Many histo-

rians believe that if he had thought more about politics and less about sex, Caesar might never have been murdered.

Mark Antony, who succeeded Caesar in the eastern half of the Roman Empire, likewise put sex ahead of politics when he met Cleopatra three years later. Instead of carrying out a planned campaign against the Parthians, he remained with Cleopatra in Egypt, giving her twins and marrying her in an Egyptian ceremony. Like Caesar, he eventually returned to Rome amid considerable criticism, but he weathered the storm by marrying Octavia, the sister of his chief rival, Octavian. Several years later, however, Antony abandoned her and reunited with Cleopatra, forming kingdoms for Caesarion and the twins, and practically inviting Octavian to avenge his sister's honor.

Octavian did just that in 33 B.C., engaging Antony and Cleopatra in the Battle of Actium, which ended inconclusively after Cleopatra inexplicably withdrew her fleet and Antony abandoned his men to sail after her. Octavian then invaded Egypt, where he encountered little resistance from the few soldiers who had not already deserted Antony. To escape from Octavian's wrath, Cleopatra started a rumor that she had taken her own life; and when a humiliated and despairing Antony heard the news, he fell on his sword, a victim of his desire for the Egyptian queen.

Strange Fruit

Seven hundred years later, sovereigns around the world were still being driven more by their hormones than by their common sense. In China, Emperor Ming-huang was famous for maintaining a harem of forty thousand concubines. One of them, Yang Kuei-fu, proved so irresistible that her every wish literally became a royal command; to satisfy her yen for litchi nuts, for instance, the emperor kept an army of horsemen continually employed in making the three-thousand-mile (4,800km) round-trip necessary to secure the exotic fruit, which is native to southern China. Despite the emperor's devotion, Yang Kuei-fu unwisely took another lover who ultimately caused her death and forced the emperor to renounce his throne.

Secret Marriages, Secret Murders

From the beginning of English history, royal lust has often rocked the empire. During the fifteenth century, the uncommonly handsome and debonair King Edward IV temporarily lost his throne after he allowed desire to prevail over politics. A man "licentious in the extreme...[who] pursued with no discrimination the married and unmarried, the noble and lowly," he unaccountably fell in love with Elizabeth Woodville Grey, an enchanting mother of two whose husband had been killed fighting against the king's forces.

According to Dominic Mancin, a contemporary chronicler, "when Edward placed a dagger at her throat, to make her submit to his passion, she remained unperturbed and determined to die rather than live unchastely with the king. Whereupon Edward coveted her much the more, and he judged the lady worthy to be a royal spouse." A short time later, Edward married the incorruptible Elizabeth. The king kept his marriage a secret for five months, only divulging the truth to prevent his court from arranging a marriage for him with a French princess.

His family and supporters were outraged to learn of his marriage, mainly because Edward was determined to support his new wife's enormous extended family. Generally, the income he provided flowed to his in-laws either through peerages created especially for them, or through marriages arranged to their advantage; the most notorious of these made Elizabeth's sixteen-year-old brother the husband of Edward's sixty-five-year-old aunt.

Nine years after Edward's accession, his brother and his closest adviser had become so jealous of the Woodvilles' influence that they forced Edward to flee England for his life; although he regained the throne the following year, lingering resentment against his in-laws inspired another brother to imprison the Woodvilles and, it is suspected, to murder Edward's two young sons and heirs.

Edward secretly married Elizabeth Grey, the widow of one of his former enemies, after she refused to become his mistress. Their marriage was later invalidated and their children declared illegitimate by Richard III, who usurped the throne after Edward's death.

Two-time Loser

Queen Elizabeth I, daughter of the often married and seldom satisfied Henry VIII, never took a spouse, but she endangered her reign through a sexual attachment to an inappropriate partner. Although she had determined while still in her teens that she would never marry—"I should call the wedding-ring the yoke-ring," she once said—she was a sensual young woman who clearly relished the company of attractive men.

Elizabeth's first brush with scandal occurred soon after her coronation in 1558. The first favorite she selected after she became queen was the handsome Lord Dudley, to whom she gave a bedchamber next to her own. Two years later, his wife was found with a broken neck at the foot of a stone staircase in her home near Oxford, and soon it was rumored that Elizabeth had had Dudley's wife murdered in order to wed him herself. Alarmed by talk of a revolution, Elizabeth decided not to marry Dudley after all, and slashed to bits the papers she had planned to sign that would have elevated him to the peerage as Earl of Leicester.

In 1554 Elizabeth became enamored of another dashing courtier, Sir Walter Raleigh. After studying at Oriel College in Oxford, he had come to court in hope of finding favor with the young queen. On a window pane that she would be sure to notice, he wrote, "Fain would I climb, yet fear to fall." With characteristic acerbity, she answered, "If thy heart fail thee, climb not at all." Yet according to one of her courtiers, she nonetheless "began to be taken with his elocution, and loved to hear his reasons for her demands. And the

truth is, she took him for a kind of oracle." In the end, however, Raleigh's heart did indeed fail him, and Elizabeth never forgave him; indeed, when she learned nearly forty years later that he had been secretly married, she had him thrown into the Tower of London.

Having given her heart twice without any hope of requital—and at the peril of her reign—Elizabeth continued to entertain marriage proposals from royalty throughout Europe while assiduously cultivating a new image for herself: that of a virgin queen who had chosen a spiritual union with all of England over marriage to a flesh-and-blood man. To reinforce this new persona, she accumulated a wardrobe of white and silver gowns encrusted with jewels, and took to the road, sleeping in more beds around her kingdom than any other monarch in British history. To the end, however, she remained a coquette, wearing an enormous red wig and stuffing fabric under her lips to fill in for her missing teeth.

✠

Elizabeth's *first brush* with scandal occurred soon after her coronation.

✠

Elizabeth *(top)* was adept at using her femininity to gain services from the men of her court, and effectively manipulated foreign rulers by virtue of her marriageability. Sir Walter Raleigh *(above)* was one of those who benefited from favor with the queen, who funded his explorations in the New World, though he later fell from grace and was imprisoned by Elizabeth.

Courtiers in Drag

The duke of Buckingham, the charming George Villiers *(above),* began his career at court as a gentleman of the king's bedchamber. Robert Carr, earl of Somerset *(right),* once served as a page to James I, but was dismissed. James and Somerset later renewed their acquaintance at a tournament, and Somerset rose rapidly in the king's favor.

James & Steenie

Steenie, the pet name given to Buckingham by James I, derived from St. Stephen, who was said in the bible to have had the "face of an angel." In 1617, James I declared to his council, "I love the Earl of Buckingham more than anyone, and more than you who are here assembled...Jesus Christ did the same and therefore I cannot be blamed. Christ had his John and I have my George."

These excerpts are from letters from James I to his son, Charles, and Buckingham, written when the pair traveled abroad:

"My Sweet Boys...I have no more to say, but that I wear Steenie's picture in a blue ribbon under my waistcoat, next to my heart. And so God bless you both, & send you a joyful & happy return...your dear dad & true friend."

"My Sweet Babie...I pray God that, after a happy conclusion there, ye may both make a comfortable & happy return in the arms of your dear dad. James R."

Lust was an even greater threat to the reign of Elizabeth's cousin and successor, James I, whose dependence on several favorites—all of them men—was but one of many personality traits his subjects found offensive. Dubbed "the wisest fool in Christendom," he ascended the throne in 1603, utterly convinced of the divine right of kings; by his lights, "Kings are not only God's lieutenants, and sit upon God's throne, but even by God himself are called God's." He further challenged

James I allowed his passion for young men to cloud his judgment, particularly in his later years when, at the insistence of the earl of Buckingham and his own son Charles, he led the country into an ill-advised war with Spain.

Parliament's authority by marveling aloud that his ancestors had ever allowed such an institution to come into existence, and argued constantly with its members over foreign policy and his own extravagance. James was at odds with his Catholic subjects as well, particularly after the Catholic Guy Fawkes confessed to an unsuccessful plot to blow up the king and his family at the House of Lords in 1605. He was on no better terms with some of his Protestant subjects, known as Puritans, who fled to America rather than remain on English soil.

But no matter how much controversy these conflicts engendered, it was James's relationship with his favorites, Robert Carr, earl of Somerset, and George Villiers, duke of Buckingham, that rocked his kingdom. According to a contemporary chronicler, these minions "like burning-glasses were daily interposed between him and the subject, multiplying the heat of oppressions in the generall opinion...the love the King shewed was as amorously conveyed as if he had mistaken their sex, and thought them ladies; which I have seene Sommerset and Buckingham labour to resemble, in the effiminatenesse of their dressings."

Buckingham, a married young courtier who had an uncanny knack for making the king laugh, was his preferred companion. The two traded letters often, with Buckingham signing his "Your most humble slave and dog, Steenie," and the king addressing him as "Sweet Heart." Indeed, Buckingham was present at the king's deathbed, where he administered a new medicine that only made James's condition worse; and he was also by his side when the king swooned and died of a stroke.

Here Comes the Sun King

But among Anne's royal contemporaries, the most famous devotees of sexual pleasure outside marriage were France's Sun King, Louis XIV, and his great-grandson and heir, Louis XV. Despite their well-deserved reputations for debauchery—the number of women they slept with is innumerable—like Anne, they practiced serial adultery, preferring to maintain intimate relationships with one favorite at a time despite the almost unlimited opportunities for extramarital sex they enjoyed.

Louis XIV began his reign of fifty-four years on March 10, 1661, having earlier married the Infanta Maria-Theresa, the short, swarthy daughter of Philip IV of Spain, in order to solidify a peace treaty between the two countries. Although Maria-Theresa loved him deeply, the Sun King did not return her affections, preferring hunting, gambling, and even statecraft to her dull company. His relationships with his four official favorites, on the other hand, were far more sexually charged—he fathered no fewer than twelve illegitimate children among the favorites. His love affairs were also far more intimate than his marriage, as he shared with his mistresses both his body and his soul.

The first of his favorites was Louise de la Baume-Leblac, whom Louis made duchess de La Vallière. Before they became lovers, she had been a lady-in-waiting to his sister-in-law, with whom he had previously enjoyed a liaison so scandalous it had threatened his monarchy. Contemporary chroniclers disagreed

TORN BETWEEN TWO LOVERS

Sarah confronts the queen about her affair with Abigail Masham, who cowers behind Anne.

The Affairs of Brandy Nan

James's great-granddaughter, Queen Anne, was also ruled by lust—but her preferred partners were women. So stout that she had to be carried to her coronation on a sedan chair, she was known popularly as "Brandy Nan" for her predilection for spirits, a taste she may have developed to help assuage her grief over seventeen disastrous pregnancies and the death of her only surviving child at age eleven.

At any rate, Anne is believed to have found more lasting comfort in the arms of Sarah Churchill, with whom the queen became infatuated even before she married Prince George of Denmark. Mistress of the queen's robes, Sarah cast a spell on Anne thought to have been stronger than that of any king's mistress in English history. In fact, Anne's desire for Sarah was so strong that she refused to dismiss her even after Sarah's husband, then earl of

Marlborough, was imprisoned in the Tower of London for intriguing against Anne's predecessor and brother-in-law, King William. Several years later, no doubt at Sarah's urging, the queen elevated Marlborough to a duke, presented the couple with a royal estate in Oxfordshire, and discharged the duke's political enemies, including her own uncle.

When Anne finally dismissed Sarah, it was to pursue another lesbian affair—this time with the beautiful Abigail Masham, a lady-in-waiting whom Sarah's political enemies supposedly planted in the household to attract the queen. Their alleged liaison was not as long-lived because Anne, the last Stuart ruler, died three years later, in 1714, suffering from alcoholism, gout, and porphyria, a genetic blood disease that is believed to have wrecked the health of her descendants as well.

While Louis XIV was kind to his chosen wife, his cousin the Infanta Maria-Theresa, he was notoriously adulterous. He pursued countless women throughout his reign, but he had four significant favorites, (clockwise from left) Madame de Montespan, the duchess de Fontages, the duchess de La Vallière, and Madame de Maintenon.

strongly as to whether La Vallière was beautiful or unattractive, but her magnetic effect on the king was indisputable—until she delivered his fourth child, and Louis took a new favorite, the beautiful marquise de Montespan. After Louis humiliated La Vallière by ordering her to share a house with her rival, La Vallière left the court and entered a convent, leaving the field free for de Montespan. She, in turn, reigned as the king's favorite for years, producing seven children. These children were legitimized, and some married into France's wealthiest families.

But de Montespan, too, was displaced by a beautiful younger woman, in this case the eighteen-year-old duchess de Fontages, who came to court specifically to seduce the king. After bearing him a son, who died after only a month, de Fontages took ill herself. Poison was the suspected agent, and the marquise de Montespan was the woman suspected of having administered it. This was an especially damning charge, since at the time some 150 noblemen and women were incarcerated on charges of having murdered, or plotted to murder, assorted spouses, children, lovers, and enemies—all by means of poison. Although the king ultimately allowed de Montespan to resume her former position, she was soon ousted a second and final time. The only surprise was the identity of her successor.

Born in prison, where her parents had been remanded for their religious beliefs, Madame de Maintenon was undoubtedly the least likely of the king's favorites: once a ravishing young girl, her looks had been ruined by a life of constant toil. She was left penniless when her elderly husband, poet Paul Scarron, whom she married at seventeen, died. She withdrew to a convent until she came to court as governess to the king's illegitimate brood with de Montespan. Nonetheless, de Maintenon was the first among equals, having married the king morganatically upon the death of his much abused wife. Moreover, de Maintenon wielded the greatest influence on the nation of any of the king's favorites: it was she who urged him to undertake France's disastrous attack on Protestants, an act that led not only to a mass persecution and exodus, but also to war with England, Spain, Russia, Holland, and Sweden, among others.

The Sins of the Great-grandfather...

Louis XV, who succeeded Louis XIV to the throne in 1715, shared with his great-grandfather a passion for procreation and a preference for serial adultery. At fifteen, he married the twenty-three-year-old Princess Marie of Poland, who bore him ten children in ten years before refusing to fulfill any further marital obligations. By his own lights, Louis was thus forced into committing adultery, and the first official favorites he selected—the four de Nesle sisters, with whom he apparently slept in sequence—indicated a decided taste for scandal even at the age of twenty-five.

Indifferent to criticism from either the clergy or the aristocracy, Louis selected as his next favorites women who went on to yield enormous power at court. The first was a bourgeoise named Jeanne Poisson whom Louis later elevated to marquise de Pompadour—a woman who remains famous today not only for her sybaritic tastes, but also for her insistence on the king's patronage of the leading architects and artists of the age. Ten years into her nineteen-year reign, she took on another role as well, acting as a spy for Empress Maria Theresa of Austria, who wanted to sign a peace treaty with France after years of warfare. Although the treaty led immediately to war with England and

Although he began his reign as "Louis the Well-Beloved," Louis's popularity waned as he recklessly indulged his appetite for sex.

Prussia, de Pompadour remained a fixture at court, retaining her hold over the king by procuring for him an endless stream of other lovers.

After her death in 1764, Louis took a new favorite, Jeanne Bécu, whom he met in 1768 at a gambling house for the nobility where she was employed as a hostess. Instantly smitten, he married her off to Comte du Barry in a vain effort to improve her social standing; then he installed her in apartments directly above his own at Versailles. Already scandalized by his liaison with Madame de Pompadour, the nobility were outraged by the king's indulgence of his new favorite: every day the comtesse du Barry was permitted to buy new dresses and diamonds, a practice that over five years cost the treasury the equivalent of sixty million dollars. Jeanne also fostered strife within the court by intriguing against various of Louis's appointees. Despite her constant conflicts with both the king's chief minister and heir, Louis kept the comtesse by his side until five days before his death in 1774, when he sent her away as a sign of penitence. She survived him by nearly twenty years, until she was sent to the guillotine along with her one-time enemies within the royal family.

A Stable of Lovers

Catherine endured seventeen years of an unhappy marriage before being liberated by her husband's murder.

In Russia, even those rulers whose names have become synonymous with lust practiced serial adultery, taking one favorite at a time, whose reigns sometimes lasted for years and whose influence helped shape the destiny of their nation. Catherine the Great was once known throughout the world for her voracious appetite for ideas. Today, she is remembered best for her voracious appetite for sex, an obsession so strong that some believe she counted stallions among her many sexual conquests. Whether out of delicacy or uncertainty, historians of the empress's reign say only that she loved to ride horses—albeit astride, like a man. But they are far more forthcoming when it comes to delineating the scandalous affairs that established her reputation.

Catherine was born in Prussia into one of the country's least-influential ruling families and was brought to Russia in 1744 to marry Empress Elizabeth's heir, the Grand Duke Peter. Sickly, scarred by smallpox, petty, and probably mentally defective, Peter was an instant and abject failure as a husband and his lonely fifteen-year-old bride soon turned to other men for comfort and pleasure.

The first men who seized her interest were historians whose books she devoured like delectable candies. Unlike other female monarchs of her time, Catherine was fascinated by philosophers, and she correspondenced with leading European intellectuals throughout her reign.

But while these distant heroes occupied her mind, Catherine had a passionate physical nature that also demanded gratification. Her first long-term lover was Sergei Saltykov, chamberlain of her husband's court, who is believed to have fathered her son Paul, born nine years after her marriage. The longtime lover who replaced him, Grigory Orlov, was also attractive and highly intelligent, and he was an eminently useful lover as well: it was he who alleged-

ly masterminded the coup and assassination that eventually enabled Catherine to wrest the throne from her husband. In addition, he fathered three of the empress's other children.

But the love of Catherine's life was Prince Grigory Potemkin, an officer of the Horse Guards who was ten years younger than she. They first met when Catherine was involved with Orlov, and their instant, mutual attraction was so striking that Orlov's brothers subsequently beat the young Potemkin so severely that he lost an eye. As soon as she and Orlov parted for good, Catherine summoned Potemkin to court and their legendary affair commenced. Although physically unattractive, the prince beguiled Catherine with his wit and wide range of intellectual pursuits. Moreover, he had the wealth and the vision required to reinforce Catherine's sense of herself as a historic personage.

In 1787, for example, he took the empress and her courtiers on an extended tour of her recently acquired Crimean territories. To ensure her comfort en route, the prince provided new furniture and even new houses to the local governors with whom she stayed. What's more, he ordered the construction of simulated villages, complete with villagers who had been instructed to wave and shout as the czarina drove past, so that Catherine would never feel anything less than regal even in the most remote regions of her empire. Three weeks later, when the party reached Kiev, Potemkin provided all the foreign ambassadors with luxurious palaces to lodge in, along with sumptuous coaches and horses; and when it was time to set sail for the Black Sea, they embarked on a flotilla of boats built especially for the occasion by the prince.

Catherine soon grew dependent on this genius of a lover, and even after their sexual relationship ceased, she consulted him about every aspect of state affairs. Sensuous and unrestrained by conventional mores, Catherine began to assemble a roster of young men, and she relied on him to procure the sexual partners she continued to crave. Indeed, Potemkin superintended a stable of some fifteen lovers for Catherine, receiving a large commission for each one. Once a prospective lover had passed muster, he was named an adjutant general and given an apartment beneath Catherine's. Whenever his services were required, he could count on finding one thousand rubles in one of Catherine's drawers; in addition, he could count on a monthly salary of some twelve thousand rubles plus expenses.

Catherine continued to rely on Potemkin to *procure* the sexual partners she *craved*.

Desires—and Children— Run Rampant

In Germany, too, lust was practically an epidemic among the royal families that ruled its eight hundred loosely confederated territories. The elector of Saxony, for example, had 354 children by an unknown number of paramours, and in neighboring dominions his fellow rulers did their best to follow his example: marrying for the sake of political expediency and then possessing as many women as they desired.

Whatever Lola Wants

King Ludwig I of Bavaria was typical of his peers, albeit considerably more flamboyant. An ugly redhead with a bad stammer, he lived in Italy for ten years before he ascended the throne in 1825, visiting museums and studios and accumulating a vast collection of artworks. His most famous collection was the "Gallery of Beauties" he established at his palace in Munich. Encompassing some thirty portraits of his mistresses, both royal and humble, it was an audacious display of his passion for sex outside marriage. Eventually, however, his lifelong devotion to lust rocked his empire so strongly that he was forced by the nobility to abdicate his throne. The cause of his downfall was not so much his illicit liaison with the mysterious Spanish dancer Lola Montez, but rather his decision to make her a countess. To

the famously snobbish Bavarian nobility, such a brazen breach of etiquette was far more alarming than mere adultery. After Louis's March 1848 abdication, Montez was forced to flee the country.

Though she claimed to be a Spanish dancer, Lola Montez (*above, left*) was born Marie Dolores Eliza Rosanna Gilbert in Limerick, Ireland. A seventeenth-century German cartoon (*above*) reflects the mood on the continent after Ludwig I created Montez countess of Landsfeld.

Victoria Regis

During this same period in England, royal lust found perhaps its most surprising expression in the history of the monarchy anywhere in the world. Although she reigned in an age distinguished by its seemingly slavish devotion to decorum, Queen Victoria was apparently beset by as many ungovernable desires as her subjects—including lust for her Scottish servant John Brown, whom some believe she married after the death of her consort, Prince Albert, in 1861.

That Victoria could have been deeply in love with an earthy representative of the lower orders still comes as a shock to those who are familiar only with the stern, even dour, public persona that she affected after Albert's death. Indeed, it seemed to many of her subjects that Victoria retired permanently from public life after this tragedy, and in many ways they were right: in the forty years that she reigned alone, she came to London only a few times, mainly to unveil memorials to Albert. She preferred instead the isolation of her private Scottish estate, Balmoral. But whatever other reasons might have led to this self-imposed seclusion, her passionate attachment to John Brown was clearly among the most significant.

A hard-drinking, plain-speaking man, Brown exerted enormous influence on the queen, particularly after he became responsible for relaying—or withholding—all messages from her family and the court. As a result, he became the object of a great deal of envy, which Victoria apparently ignored. Indeed, she was so enamored of Brown that she allowed him to address her as "Woman" even in the presence of others; and more tellingly, in a letter to his mother after his death, Victoria recalled how "often and often I told him no one loved him more than I did or had a better friend than me: and he answered 'Nor you—than me.'" Among the many instructions the queen left for her own death, one was for Brown to place her body in its coffin. Of course, her adored lover—and possible husband—was unable to fulfill her request, but she had left others as well: most notably, that a photo of Brown was to be laid near her heart and a lock of his hair was to be placed in her left hand.

Last Request

Queen Victoria's "instructions" for her burial were reportedly from a hand-written note:

In case of the Queen's death she wishes that her faithful and devoted personal attendant (and true friend) John Brown should be in the room and near at hand, and that he should watch over her earthly remains and place it in the coffin, with Lohlein [Prince Albert's valet] or, failing, one who may be most generally in personal attendance on her. This her Physicians are to explain in case of necessity to those of her children who may be there.

From the diary of Sir James Reid, the queen's personal physician:

24 January 1901: I had a talk with Mrs. Tuck [the Queen's chief dresser] who, the night before, had read me the Queen's instructions about what the Queen had ordered her to put in the coffin, some of which none of the family were to see...Later I helped her and the nurse to put a satin dressing gown and garter ribbon and star, etc. on the Queen. We cut off her hair to be put into lockets, and rearranged the flowers.

25 January 1901: At 9:30 I went to the Queen's room, and arranged with Mrs. Tuck and Miss Stewart to put on the floor of the Queen's coffin, over the layer of charcoal 1 1/2 inches thick, the various things (dressing gown of Prince Consort, a cloak of his embroidered by Princess Alice, the Prince Consort's plaster hand, numerous photographs, etc.) which Her Majesty had left instructions with them to put in...Then I packed the sides with bags of charcoal in muslin and put in the Queen's left hand the photo of Brown and his hair in a case (according to her private instructions) which I wrapped in tissue paper, and covered with Queen Alexandra's flowers.

Rumors about the queen and her servant John Brown circulated after the prince consort's death.

Royal Appetites

Queen Victoria's son Bertie, later King Edward VII, made the pursuit of pleasure his life's work after it became clear that his long-lived mother would never provide him with any meaningful employment at court. "I don't mind praying to the eternal father," he once joked, "but I must be the only man in the country afflicted with an eternal mother."

Though he indulged his appetites for food, tobacco, and gambling, it was to his passion for sex that Bertie was truly devoted. In fact, some biographers believe that he was actually addicted to sex, estimating that he bedded more than seven thousand women in his lifetime, beginning with a German girl he allegedly forced to satisfy him in public when he was only fifteen years old.

As he matured, his obsession flourished, encompassing some of Europe's most celebrated beauties, as well as Parisian prostitutes who attended him in an armchair built especially to accommodate girls who were, as he put it, "good on their knees." Yet like so many royals before him, neither his marriage to Princess Alexandra of Denmark nor his compulsive coupling with virtual strangers prevented him from maintaining equable relationships with a series of favorites.

One, Lillie Langtry, was the world's first "professional beauty"; her career was launched after a portrait of her created a sensation at the Royal Academy. Although Lillie's husband often threatened to sue her for divorce and name Bertie as co-respondent, it was another of Bertie's favorites—Lady Mordaunt—whose indiscretions did the first widespread damage to Bertie's reputation.

Though Bertie remained married to Alexandra for forty-seven years, like other monarchs he took a series of mistresses. Among the most celebrated was the sultry actress Lillie Langtry *(above)*, who was known as the "Jersey Lily."

Sued for divorce by her husband on grounds of adultery, Lady Mordaunt confessed her guilt and implicated Bertie by entering into evidence twelve letters he had written to her. Although the notes were harmless, Lady Mordaunt was shipped off to an insane asylum to prevent further scandal. Afterward, joked a palace insider, "London was black with the smoke of burnt confidential letters."

Bertie continued his affairs, causing another scandal when, at the age of fifty, he became infatuated with Frances "Daisy" Brooke, whose former lover maliciously publicized Daisy's liaison with the king.

When Bertie was near death, his last favorite, the Honorable Mrs. Alice Keppel, revealed a letter written by Bertie ten years earlier, assuring her that she would be welcome at his side should he ever take ill. Bowing to her husband's apparent wishes, Alexandra allowed her rival to enter the king's sickroom, but within minutes Keppel had fled in tears; to this day no one knows what passed between the two women. The distraught queen was unwilling to leave the corpse of her much-loved, though highly flawed husband, wailing "They want to take him away but I can't bear to part with him. Once they hide his face from me everything is gone forever."

Princess Grace and Her Toy Boys

✠

Grace took

pains

to shield her

young lovers

from the media

even as she

trumpeted **their**

accomplishments to

members of her

inner circle.

✠

Like every bride, Her Serene Highness Princess Grace began her marriage with high hopes for enduring love and happiness, but like nearly every royal spouse in history, those hopes were soon dashed by the exigencies of royal life.

In her case, those exigencies were her husband's requirement that she devote herself entirely to her family and to Monaco. During the first years of her marriage, it seems to have been relatively easy for Grace, one of the world's finest actresses, to play this new role; but as her children grew and Rainier became increasingly involved in building Monaco's economy, the princess began to feel constrained by life within the palace walls—and isolated in her fairy-tale marriage.

Robert Dornhelm was most likely Grace's lover, though he declines to kiss and tell.

According to biographer Robert Lacey, in 1976 Grace confessed to Gwen Robyns, a fellow biographer, "I have come to feel very sad in this marriage...[Rainier] is not really interested in me. He doesn't care about me." His indifference—which he was known to display in ostentatious fits of snoozing at social events she had arranged—was especially troubling at a time when Grace's self-esteem, never very great, had already been weakened consid-

erably by the ravages of menopause on her face and figure. She called it the "angry jaws" and often referred to herself as "Blimposaurus Rex."

It was during the throes of this personal crisis that Grace met director Robert Dornhelm, a dashing European sixteen years younger than she, whom she met when she agreed to act as host for a documentary he was filming about the former Russian Imperial Ballet School. The film was eventually nominated for an Academy Award, but more important to Grace was the success of their collaboration off-screen. Although Dornhelm refuses to discuss their relationship, biographers Lacey and Robyns are confident that the two were lovers.

But Dornhelm was not, apparently, the only "toy boy" in Grace's life. In 1980, she allegedly began an affair with Jeffrey Martin FitzGerald, then a handsome, twenty-nine-year-old corporate headhunter who partied with Grace whenever she visited New York. "I thought he'd hate my bumps and lumps," the Princess reportedly confided to a friend, "but he doesn't seem to mind one bit." She took pains, however, to shield her young lovers from the media even as she trumpeted their accomplishments to members of her inner circle.

Not surprisingly, these secret relationships did not, by themselves, transform Grace back into the radiantly happy movie star who once took Monaco by storm; but they apparently did provide some much-needed consolation. By 1981, she had regained so much of her former sense of humor that she could dryly comfort a nervous Lady Diana Spencer, "Don't worry dear. It'll get worse."

Lovers' Secrets

Ironically, Bertie's scandalous relationship with Alice Keppel seems to have been weirdly reanimated in the persons of his great-grandson Charles, the current Prince of Wales, and Camilla Parker-Bowles, the great-great-granddaughter of Alice Keppel. Were their story fiction, readers would no doubt condemn it as incredible, but with each new chapter, it has become more and more evident that Charles's affair with this married woman is, like his ancestor's, the ruling passion of his life—and one that his wife, unlike Bertie's, is unable to forgive.

According to biographers, Charles first met Camilla, the daughter of one of England's wealthiest families, when he was twenty-three, before he felt ready to think seriously about marriage. Unfortunately for the prince, his friend Andrew Parker-Bowles had no such reservations, and he and Camilla were married the following year. Soon thereafter, Charles no doubt recognized his mistake; for even if he were able to convince Camilla to obtain a divorce, under British law he would be obliged to choose between ruling England and

marrying a divorcée. Since renouncing his claim to the throne was unthinkable, he apparently reconciled himself to enjoying Camilla as a mistress and burnishing his reputation as the world's most eligible bachelor.

With the announcement of his long-awaited engagement to Lady Diana Spencer, the daughter of a family friend, in 1981, most of the world leaped at the chance to luxuriate in the romance of his forthcoming nuptials. Charles, on the other hand, seemed to want nothing more than to maintain the status quo with

✠

Just days before their *wedding*, Diana reportedly threatened to *call it off* after she found an expensive bracelet that Charles had bought for Camilla and engraved with their *pet names.*

✠

Camilla—and damn the consequences. Just days before their wedding, Diana reportedly threatened to call it off after she found an expensive bracelet that Charles had bought for Camilla and engraved with their pet names. Diana's doubts reportedly resurfaced during her honeymoon, when she came across photos of Camilla that Charles had brought along.

Thereafter, according to royal biographer Peter Fearon, "Princess Diana began to do almost anything to get attention, including what have been called 'suicide' attempts. When she was three months pregnant with Prince William, she tumbled down a flight of stairs....On another occasion she is reported to have slashed her wrist....On yet another occasion she is said to have thrown herself at a glass cabinet in despair and on another to have taken a slight overdose of sleeping pills." By 1984, just three years after their marriage, Charles and Diana were reportedly maintaining separate bedrooms, separate public schedules, and separate private lives.

It is likely that very few outside the royal family would have learned about her anguish if Diana had not allowed her friends to meet with journalist Andrew Morton, who published a biography of the princess in the spring of 1992—despite efforts to suppress it. The mysterious emotional breakdowns that Morton detailed stunned a world that had grown accustomed to thinking of Diana as a heroine in a fairy tale. Everywhere, people asked the same question: what was it that had rendered the prince utterly indifferent to this gorgeous paragon who was devoted to her kids and good works?

Soon after, British intelligence reportedly began keeping the princess under surveillance, focusing their efforts on one of her closest male friends: James Gilbey, a member of the wealthy gin-distilling family. It is believed by some biographers that intelligence agents not only recorded Diana's conversations with Gilbey, but also released a tape of one of their talks, now known as the "Squidgy" tape, to a London tabloid in the summer of 1992. Throughout the conversation—which created a sensation around the world—the man said to be Gilbey refers to the woman as "Squidgy," and at one point passionately declares, "I love you, I love you, I love you."

A tape-recorded conversation rocked Buckingham Palace again in November 1992, when the Australian magazine *New Idea* published a transcript of a telephone conversation purportedly between Charles and Camilla. What shocked the public most was not the discovery that lust is Charles's ruling passion, but rather the revolting way in which he expressed his desire for his mistress on tape. For example, after assuring the woman that he needs her every week, the man said to be Charles fantasizes about living "inside your trousers or something." The woman then laughs, asking whether he intends to "come back as a pair of knickers"—to which the man replies, "Or, God forbid, a Tampax. Just my luck!...My luck to be chucked down a lavatory and go on and on forever swirling round on the top, never going down."

With the release of these tapes—and the avalanche of negative publicity they generated—Charles and Diana had little option but to authorize the British prime minister to announce their separation on December 9, 1992. A year later, Princess Diana officially retired from public life,

James Hewitt's account of his affair with Diana indicated that the princess, like her husband, resorted to extramarital sex.

and in June 1994, Prince Charles revealed on an internationally broadcast television documentary what most of the world had suspected for years—that he had, in fact, committed adultery, albeit, he claimed, after his marriage to Diana had irretrievably broken down.

It seemed, then, that all of the skeletons had finally been ferreted out of the famously capacious royal closet—until October 1994, when three new books revealed shocking details about the love lives of the prince and princess of Wales.

The first to achieve instant bestseller status was *Princess in Love,* which alleged that Diana shared her husband's passion for sex outside marriage. Based on the supposed memoirs of James Hewitt, a strikingly handsome former Life Guards officer who had once given riding lessons to Diana, the book contended that the princess seduced Hewitt in 1986 after a private dinner in Kensington Palace. Their torrid, five-year affair reportedly included at least six more passionate sex trysts in set-

tings such as pool houses, bathrooms, and the family's country home, where the lovers cavorted while Diana's sons entertained themselves in the room next door. Although Britons snatched up the book in record time, Hewitt was nonetheless branded a traitor—the *Daily Mirror,* for example, called him a "revolting creep," and opined that "horse whipping would be too good for him." Hewitt secretly fled Great Britain for a converted pigsty at an isolated farm in France, where he reportedly tried to overcome the trauma of his public humiliaton.

But the scandal surrounding Diana's alleged adultery only deepened after a British tabloid reported that a former Royal Marines commander claimed to have been ordered to videotape a partially clad man and a woman making love in James Hewitt's backyard—on the same night that Diana was seen arriving there in a chauffeur-driven limousine. The ex-commander was quoted as saying that his superior officer had confiscated the

videotape and ordered secrecy, a contention that led some British legislators to express renewed fears that British Intelligence was regularly spying on royals instead of protecting them.

This scandal had barely subsided when another instant bestseller made headlines around the world. Billed as an authorized biography and based on extensive interviews with Charles and his inner circle of friends and advisers, *The Prince of Wales* revealed that the prince had married Diana not for love, but because he had felt pressured by his father to protect her reputation. Far from sympathizing with the prince, who apparently confessed to friends that soon after his marriage he felt "trapped in a rather desperate cul-de-sac," most Britons were shocked by his candor, as were most of Britain's editorial writers: the *Sunday Times* of London called the book "a staggering breach of royal protocol and an affront to decent behavior," while *The People* called it "the longest abdication note in history."

Within days of the publication of *The Prince of Wales*, the Italian magazine *Voici* reported that Diana expected to receive a $35 million settlement from Charles as part of their 1995 divorce—news it had gleaned from an advance copy of yet another biography, *Diana, Her New Life.* The British press reacted to the news—and to other revelations, including the contention that Diana had once threatened to run away to Australia with her two sons—with typical acerbity, while a prominent British book-maker announced new odds on the monarchy's demise by the year 2000: 5 to 1.

Whatever the final chapter of this fairy tale–turned–soap opera, one thing is for sure: there's nothing like lust for rocking an empire.

CHAPTER THREE

Never Too Much

This eighteenth-century painting *(left)* entitled "The Royal Family" graces the walls at Versailles;
Princess Diana *(above)*, in more care-free days.

ince the beginning of history, the world's monarchs have been ruled by one passion more than any other: a passion for excess. ⚜

It was excess that compelled the earliest sovereigns to conquer new territories, enslave countless populations, murder their opponents, and seize as much sexual satisfaction from as many partners as possible. ⚜

More recent monarchs have eschewed violence for public relations, but their aim has remained unchanged: to fulfill their every fantasy, no matter how bizarre or dangerous. ⚜

Still others have sought to indulge their outsized egos by commissioning extraordinary works of art and architecture intended to glorify their reigns or by declaring themselves the arbiters of taste. ⚜ But the monarchs who have always captured our imagination most completely are those who found the fullest expression for excess through violence and madness. ⚜

The Savage Duke

In Renaissance Italy Galeazzo Maria Sforza, the duke of Milan, was the most infamous of several rulers whose madness evinced itself through acts of pathological cruelty. Among his sadistic crimes was the rape of untold numbers of high-born Milanese ladies, whose husbands and fathers were then forced to suffer in silence while the duke described his depredations in excruciating detail. Once, when an astrologer predicted that he would not survive the

Transgressors were **tortured** and mutilated by the duke with *his* **bare hands.**

eleventh year of his reign, Galeazzo had him locked in a dungeon with a loaf of bread, a capon wing, and a glass of wine—and then left him to starve to death. On another occasion, after he captured a poacher who had illegally trapped a hare, Galeazzo ordered the man to eat the animal whole, including its eyes, bones, fur, and entrails; needless to say, the wretch died soon thereafter. Other transgressors were tortured and mutilated by the duke with his bare hands.

Galeazzo Maria's bloody rule ended with his assassination in 1476 by republican conspirators who spent days stabbing one another with sheathed daggers to rehearse their crime. After his death, Galeazzo's wife ruled as regent until their son, Gian Galeazzo, came of age.

The king *was inadvertently* *set afire* *during* a masked ball *and, while he managed* **to escape** serious *injury,* the incident **triggered** another bout of **insanity.**

Episodes of Insanity

King Charles VI of France was also mad, though never knowingly cruel. Born to notoriously unstable parents, he succeeded to the throne as a child in 1380; twelve years later, he went insane during a routine military mission, killing four of his men-at-arms for no apparent reason. After being bound and pinioned, he was taken to Le Mans to recover and was able to resume his duties. But soon thereafter, the king was inadvertently set afire during a masked ball; while he managed to escape serious physical injury, the incident triggered another bout of insanity. From then on Charles was plagued by episodes of madness, a condition that was no doubt worsened by his wife's very public affair with her brother-in-law.

The Last of the Lancasters

Charles's grandson, King Henry VI of England, apparently inherited his ancestors' mental instability; indeed, he

Henry's mental incompetence put great power in the hands of those who could influence him, leading to vicious struggles for control and eventually to Henry's murder in the Tower of London.

was often so incapacitated that he was incapable of ruling his kingdom. An unusually humble young king—he preferred the round-toed shoes of a farmer and the hooded gown of a townsman to royal raiments—he was also exceptionally pious, and made a vow after his marriage to Margaret to never so much as look unchastely at another woman.

But by 1450, Henry's oddities had begun to alarm his court, and his political enemies began urging his abdication. Three years later he suffered a breakdown so severe that for seventeen months he was unable to recognize friends or to understand that his wife had given birth to their son. After suffering a second breakdown in 1455, both Henry and his son were murdered, and he became the last of the Lancastrians to rule England.

In the Company of Angels

King George III of England was likewise beset by mental problems, now known to have been caused by porphyria inherited from his Hanoverian ancestors. Known as "Farmer George" for his rustic tastes, habits of frugality, and enormous family, he was overcome by his first attack of lunacy in 1788. According to writer Fanny Burney, joint keeper of the queen's robes, the king spoke with a

Xenophobic Decrees

George III is shown here wearing a Windsor uniform, in 1812, the fifty-second year of his reign. By this time George's illness had progressed to the point that his son, the Prince of Wales, who later succeeded him as George IV, had been named regent.

Czar Paul of Russia is likewise believed to have inherited the unstable tendencies of his ancestors, most notably those of his father Peter, who was deposed and later assassinated by command of Paul's mother, Catherine the Great. As a child, Paul suffered keenly from his mother's hostility and neglect, and as a young man he began displaying the symptoms of mental illness that had also blighted his father's life. He told friends that Peter the Great had appeared to him in a dream to warn him of an early death, and he was so suspicious of his mother that he established his own private army. But not even his mother's death and his own coronation in 1796 could keep his paranoia in check.

Like many monarchs suffering from mental illness, Paul sought to allay his anxieties by fiat, issuing decrees that few of his subjects dared defy. Obsessed by a fear of foreign influences, he forbade Russians from leaving the country to study or travel in Europe and banned all foreign music and books. Later, he decreed that anyone found wearing French boots, coats, or hats would be summarily fined, arrested, or exiled, while anyone suspected of harboring "nefarious thoughts" would be banished to Siberia. Banishment was also the fate of any Russian who failed to kneel before the czar or his palaces—even if the offender was on horseback or in a carriage. After four years of increasingly lunatic rule, Paul was murdered by his closest advisers, and his son, who was aware of the plot, was installed in his place.

"rapidity, a hoarseness of voice, a volubility, an earnestness—a vehemence, rather—it startled me inexpressibly... Heaven preserve him! The Queen grows more and more uneasy." As the days passed the king became even more manic, talking so incessantly that he became delirious and began foaming at the mouth. It was even reported that he had gotten out of his coach in Windsor Great Park to shake hands with an oak tree, believing it to be Frederick the Great.

After a brief recovery, George was once again overcome by illness in 1801 and went blind four years later; in 1811, he suffered his final breakdown after learning of the death of his favorite daughter Amelia, and retired to Windsor Castle. There, wrote Fanny Burney, "The beloved King is in the best state possible for his present melancholy situation; that is, wholly free from real bodily suffering, or imaginary mental misery, for he is persuaded that he is always conversing with angels."

Chinese Construction on a Grand Scale

From the dawn of its first dynasty, imperial China was ruled by emperors who understood instinctively that no victory in battle would secure their thrones as surely as the awe-inspiring monuments to themselves that they regularly commissioned. Thus the first emperor, Ch'in Shih Huang-ti, had no qualms about forcing some 700,000 prisoners to build nearly three hundred palaces in the second century B.C., each filled with treasures and statuary. The object of this enterprise was not merely to provide the emperor with appropriately sumptuous accommodations, but also to impress the populace on a daily basis with his ubiquity.

As fabulous as they were, these palaces were insignificant when compared with the emperor's most famous

China's Great Wall is a landmark of a magnitude its builder could not have foreseen— the wall is visible even from space.

memorial to his own majesty: the Great Wall of China, which still stretches for fourteen hundred miles (2,240km) across China. Twelve years in the making, it was also the tomb of the 500,000 laborers who perished while constructing it.

Eight hundred years later, Emperor Yang-ti was responsible for the construction of another enduring Chinese monument: a nine-hundred-mile (1,440km) waterway connecting the valleys of the Yellow and Yangtze Rivers. Between 605 and 610, tens of thousands of peasants were forced to labor on this enterprise so that the emperor could enjoy his fleet of forty thousand boats. One of his greatest pleasures was watching the sometimes sixty (96km)-mile-long procession of pleasure crafts that would precede his own magnificent ship on cruises down the waterway. In rainy weather or high winds, thousands of soldiers would pull the emperor's boat with strong ropes, so that his progress was never impeded.

A Fondness for Metalwork

In 724, the neighboring Japanese emperor Shomu forced thousands of peasants to participate in the construction of his pet project: a Buddhist monastery complete with an enormous statue of Buddha. Every bronze object in the kingdom was melted down for use in the fifty-three-foot (16.1m) -high monument, which was built in forty-one stages over a period of two years; another eighteen months of work was required for casting the 966 curls that adorn the Buddha's head. Altogether, one million pounds (454,000kg) of metal and five hundred pounds (227kg) of gold were needed to complete the finished statue, which was consecrated in a religious ceremony led by ten thousand priests.

But the most extravagant builder of monuments to himself was Hideyoshi, the most powerful shogun to dominate the Japanese national politics during the six-

Hideyoshi, the "Napoleon of Japan," who amassed great political power and fabulous wealth, was born a peasant.

teenth century. Unlike many of his predecessors, Hideyoshi was both fabulously wealthy and enormously vain, and he was consumed by a passion for excess. His most lavish conceit was a castle, built in Osaka, that was distinguished by 125 towers and surrounded by two rings of impregnable walls spread across two hundred acres (80ha). According to one historian, "virtually everything he would have to touch he ordered in gold—his bowls, his chopsticks, the locks on his doors, the latches on the windows. Nothing was exempt from his passion for display. A visitor lamented, 'The very privies are decorated with gold and silver, and paintings in fine colors. All the precious things are used as if they were dirt.'"

From Hunting Lodge to Glittering Showplace

A century later in France, King Louis XIV established an even greater reputation for conspicuous consumption at his palace of Versailles. His father, King Louis XIII, had hunted in Versailles as a child, and recalled the experience with such fondness that in 1624 he purchased 117 acres (46.8ha) of land near the village, and constructed a twenty-six-room chateau of brick, stone, and slate. Delighted by the relative informality of his new hunting lodge, Louis XIII purchased the entire village of Versailles in 1632 and began renovating the chateau while adding pavilions and enhancing the park that surrounded it.

Louis XIV was five when he succeeded his father to the throne, and grew up in an atmosphere of unparalleled luxury and unremitting insecurity. The former he regarded as his by divine right, while the latter he attributed to the overarching ambitions of the French nobility. While still in his youth, he decided to dedicate his life to indulging his own passion for excess, while curbing the excesses of his court, and it was at Versailles that he achieved his twin desires.

After visiting this rustic retreat in 1661, Louis too succumbed to its charms, and decided to follow his father's example by putting into practice there his ideas about art and architecture—on a scale in keeping with his love of luxury. Forty-two years later his monument to his own majesty was finally complete, thanks to the efforts of a virtual army of architects, artisans, laborers, and gardeners—as many as twenty-two thousand worked at Versailles on a daily basis—who had no choice but to fulfill the king's dream of building the world's most magnificent royal residence.

Louis Le Vau was chief architect to Louis XIV and the genius behind many of the reconstructions at Versailles.

✠

Louis decided to **dedicate** his life to *indulging* his **passion** for **excess.**

✠

Louis's palatial bedroom at Versailles is truly fit for a Sun King.

The nobility was forced to *spend* so much time and **money** at Versailles that they rarely had the opportunity to create the kind of political *turmoil* that had so **unsettled** the **king** in his youth.

The interior of Louis's architectural masterpiece was a marvel intended to ensure his glory for posterity. One of his greatest—and most extravagant—achievements was the Galerie des Glaces, an enormous gallery lined with mirrors and gold statuary that was lit at night by dozens of dazzling crystal chandeliers. Louis's bedchamber was another gem: originally the State Drawing Room, its walls were hung with heavy gold brocade, and it was decorated with rock crystals and marbles to reflect light from tall windows with gilded frames. Nowhere else in the world did a monarch sleep in such sumptuous quarters.

It should come as no surprise, then, that at Versailles Louis also established the monarchy's most elaborate court etiquette to date, one which practically deified the ruler known throughout his reign as the Sun King. Every moment of his day was choreographed both for his comfort and for the edification of the nobility; no event involving his person, from getting dressed to eating dinner, was performed either spontaneously or without the assistance of others. Indeed, whenever he went to Versailles Louis required the daily attendance of an entourage numbering fifteen thousand, including his immediate family; lesser royalty and their families; the royal favorites; and officers of the state and the armed forces. In fact, the nobility were forced to spend so much time and money at Versailles that they rarely had the opportunity to visit their own estates—or to create the kind of political turmoil that had so unsettled the king in his youth.

Instead, they spent their leisure time at Versailles indulging their own considerable passions for excess. Sexual promis-cuity and homosexuality, both contrary to the morals of the age, were the norm at the palace. According to contemporary chronicler Bussy-Rabutin, the sexual availability of the noblewomen at Versailles was so pronounced that many young courtiers barely noticed them: "Debauch reigned more supremely here than any-where in the world...Wine-bibbing and the unmentionable vice were so fashion-able that...their evil example soon perverted the intentions of the more virtu-ous, so that they succumbed to the lure of viciousness."

Some courtiers went so far as to estab-lish a fraternity of misogynists whose officers were selected according to the size of their genitalia. One of their most scandalous acts, according to Bussy-Rabutin, "took place in a house of plea-sure...[where] they seized hold of one of [the courtesans], tied her wrists and ankles to the bed-posts, thrust a firework into a part of her body which decency forbids me to mention, and put a match to it." Eventually, many of these dissolute princes and nobles were exiled from the court by direct order of the king, but homosexual sex continued to be practiced at Versailles throughout Louis's reign.

One especially notorious homosexual was the king's own brother, while another was the brother of the king's favorite, de la Valliere. In his memoirs, Primi Visconti, a visitor to the palace, recalled how de la Valliere once attempted to seduce him by observing, "'Monsieur, in Spain, the monks; in France, the nobility; in Italy, everyone...' I had quite a task to extricate myself from this situation. The marquis died soon afterwards of a disease of the anus, a disease which was very wide-spread at that time."

Deposed by Excess

Charles's personal weaknesses eventually led to a trial, at which he was declared an "enemy of his people," and to his distinction as the only reigning British king to die on the scaffold.

King Charles I of England came to the throne in the seventeenth century with an aversion for the homosexual excesses of the court—his father, James I, was himself a homosexual—but with a passion for asserting his majesty through conspicuous consumption.

As a child, Charles had suffered from a speech impediment that contributed both to his lifelong shyness and to his preference for relatively solitary pleasures like scholarship. But none of his studies prepared him for the beauties of Italian art, which he encountered on a trip overseas; utterly overcome, he soon established an international reputation as a connoisseur and patron.

Indeed, even before he ascended the throne in 1625 Charles had embarked upon the first of a series of monumental building projects that would change the face of British architecture. Ordinary

Britons as well as scholars were impressed by Charles's taste and knowledge, agreeing with contemporary chronicler Lucy Hutchinson that the king was "a most excellent judge and a greate lover of paintings, carvings, gravings and many other ingenuities less offensive than the bawdry and prophane abusive witt which was the only exercise of the other Court."

But Charles's vehement opposition to Puritans—he was a Catholic—and his unshakeable belief in the divine right of kings made him the object of considerable public criticism as well. Eventually, Charles's absolutism—and his mania for collecting artworks at any expense—proved fatal. Soon after he alienated Parliament by purchasing against its wishes a collection of paintings he could ill afford, he outraged them altogether by attempting to arrest five members of the House of Commons. A civil war ensued, and five years later, in 1647, his forces were vanquished by the Puritan armies of Oliver Cromwell.

Branded "a tyrant, a traitor, a murderer and public enemy," Charles was sentenced to die on January 30, 1649, on a scaffold outside the huge banqueting hall at Whitehall that he had commissioned early in his reign—as good a place as any to execute a king reviled more than anything for his vanity. Dressed in two shirts so that he would not be seen to shiver when he was led to his death, Charles warned his executioners that he would "forgive no subject of mine who comes to shed my blood." As the axe fell, wrote contemporary chronicler Philip Henry, a boy of seventeen standing nearby heard "'such a groan as I never heard before, and desire I may never hear again.'"

THE KING'S SALAD DAYS

Guiseppe Arcimboldo's "Vertumnus," painted in 1590, was modeled after Emperor Rudolf II.

Royal Zoologist

King Augustus of Poland was also obsessed with the mysteries of the natural world—he is still famous today for having sponsored the first zoological expedition from Europe to Africa—and like his contemporaries, Charles I and Louis XIV, he spared no expense in commissioning monuments and amassing treasures intended to glorify his reign. His most famous architectural commission was a group of Baroque-style buildings known as the Zwinger, where he presided over lavish pageants and displayed an unrivaled collection of porcelains, antique sculptures, ivory carvings, Renaissance bronzes, and prints. Eventually, the business of collecting became infinitely more important to Augustus than the business of ruling, and he was vilified upon his death as a vainglorious wastrel.

Augustus's rule marked the most disastrous period in Polish history.

Objets de Nature

Elsewhere in Europe, other monarchs were likewise devoted to indulging their passion for excess—often at their peril. In Germany the Habsburg Emperor Rudolf II had become obsessed with the mysteries of the natural world, and had begun to accumulate a collection of bizarre artworks meant to explore the erotic and the magical; not surprisingly, his favorite painter was Giuseppe Arcimboldo, whose celebrated portraits were composed of fruits, vegetables, books, and other objects, arranged to resemble the subject. As Rudolf's interest in mysticism deepened, so too did his isolation from the realities of daily life—so much so that he was finally ousted from the throne by his brother Marius in 1611.

Fabergé's Eggs

One of the most impassioned royal patrons of the nineteenth century was Czar Alexander III of Russia, who inaugurated one of the world's most famous collections of curiosities: the fifty-five priceless Fabergé eggs commissioned as gifts for Easter and other occasions by the imperial family.

The Russian mania for exchanging and eating eggs at Easter reached its zenith in the 1800s, when in St. Petersburg alone some five hundred thousand people consumed more than ten million eggs. Hundreds of special markets and stalls were set up around the country to sell eggs stained red and decorated with complex designs. Confectioners sold candy and chocolate eggs as well, while other merchants offered egg-shaped boxes of paper or glass filled with flowers or wax figures.

The czars of Russia took the country's passion a step further by commissioning a series of elaborate, jeweled eggs. Forty-three of Fabergé's inimitable creations are still extant. Among the most famous is the "coronation egg," which Nicholas presented to his wife in 1897. Still another renowned treasure is the egg that the czar presented to his wife in 1907: enameled in mauve, Alexandra's favorite color, it features a four-inch (10.1cm) -high swan that can propel itself on tiny webbed feet in an aquamarine "lake." Still other famous examples of Fabergé's unrivaled craftsmanship are eggs that open to reveal clockwork models of the Trans-Siberian Express train and the imperial yacht.

Fabergé, who employed as many as seven hundred craftsmen at the height of his fame, designed these remarkable treasures for the imperial family until 1917, when the provisional government established by the Bolsheviks prevented him from meeting with the czar. In 1918 the House of Fabergé was nationalized and its contents looted; the world's most famous jeweler asked only that he be allowed to keep his hat.

The Start of the Tradition

The first Fabergé egg was presented by Alexander to his wife Marie to lift her spirits after the assassination of her father-in-law. Made of gold and white enamel, the egg opened to reveal a yolk, also made of gold, which in turn opened to reveal a tiny gold hen and a model of the imperial crown, set with a ruby. The first was such a success that the czar began ordering an egg every year at Easter, always making sure that the design was kept a secret. After Alexander's death, his son Czar Nicholas maintained the tradition, ordering eggs for his mother, as well as for his wife Alexandra.

The lilies of the valley egg is studded with photographs of the royal family.

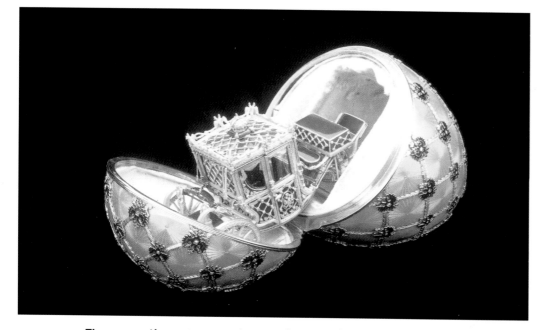

The coronation egg opens to reveal an exquisite miniature coach topped with a diadem of diamonds.

Ludwig's Fantasyland

Ludwig devoted his life to building a series of fantastic palaces in which he could *reinvent* himself as the hero of a medieval legend.

Ludwig II of Bavaria never even bothered trying to rule his kingdom; ruled himself by a passion for excess—and, some believe, by madness—he instead devoted his life to building a series of fantastic palaces in which he could reinvent himself as the hero of a medieval legend. Raised in relative isolation in an ersatz Gothic fortress built by his father, Maximilian II, Ludwig grew up in an atmosphere of unremitting theatricality and unquestioned extravagance. Only eighteen years old when he ascended the throne in 1864, he lost no time in directing the treasury to subsidize his favorite composer, Richard Wagner—an arrangement that did much to reinforce Ludwig's sense of himself as a heroic figure, but left Bavaria nearly bankrupt.

Soon thereafter, the king embarked on the first of his monuments to his own over-the-top aesthetic: the castle of Neuschwanstein, a towering neo-Gothic residence that resembled nothing so much as a theatrical dream world. His second fantasy palace, built in 1869, was even more extravagant: called Linderhof, it featured an enormous artificial grotto, illuminated by multicolored electric lights, in which he could meditate while floating on a barge. His third and most self-consciously theatrical palace, the Schloss Herrenchiemsee, was intended to replicate Versailles, but its interior decoration was so excessive that it impressed others as the work of a madman, not a visionary.

In his private life, too, Ludwig aspired to the theatrical. He made a great show of resenting his mother's Prussian roots—typically, he referred to her as "my predecessor's wife" and refused to see her in person—but he shared with his mother's family an unswerving belief in the divine right of kings. The same ambivalence characterized his attitude toward his fiancee, Elizabeth of Bavaria, whom he courted with self-conscious flamboyance before ensuring that their engagement would be broken off. Passages from Ludwig's letters and diaries point to homosexual tendencies, and some historians believe that his ambivalence toward marriage stemmed from his apparently homosexual attachment to his stablemaster, who managed the king's activities for the last seventeen years of his life.

But no one, it seems, could control the inevitable progression of the madness that finally killed him. In 1886, after nearly two decades of increasingly bizarre behavior, the king was declared officially insane—although historian Ghislain de Diesbach maintains that he was not a madman so much as "an eccentric and misanthrope who despised the human condition while still remaining desperately attached to it." It will never be known whether he was simply worn down by a lifetime devoted to re-creating the fantasy world of operas and legends, or whether he inherited the same seeds of madness that killed his uncle; in any event, less than two weeks after he was declared incompetent, Ludwig was found floating in the waters of Lake Starnberg, a probable victim of suicide.

George IV's drinking, infidelities, and extravagance made him a decidedly unpopular ruler.

The Regency's Regent

The international fame of England's King George IV exemplified a sea-change in the public perception of the monarchy and the monarchy's perception of itself—the status of royalty was diminished by the historical push toward democracy, and rulers began ensuring their place in the world by presenting themselves as unequalled models of sophistication. Said by Harold Walpole to have been "a bad son, a bad husband, a bad father, a bad subject, a bad monarch, and a bad friend," George excelled only at securing public acclaim as a style maker—a goal he pursued obsessively soon after he was declared prince regent on account of his father's madness.

Although George was famous for inspiring the Regency style of interior decoration that distinguished Carlton House, his London residence, he was not in any sense a serious student of architecture or the arts. In fact, he soon grew bored by classically inspired refinements, and redecorated the palace to resemble a Chinese pagoda. George's gaily colored pavilion at Brighton was even more fantastical in conception, distinguished by onion domes and exotic, Asian-inspired furnishings. These palaces were not intended to assert an aesthetic vision or even to reinforce the king's majesty; rather, they were designed to impress upon the public his unerring taste and sophistication.

To secure his public persona as a style maker, George took the unprecedented step of opening his lavish showplaces to a large number of Britons. After hosting an extravagant Carlton House party for three thousand aristocrats in June of 1811, he decided to invite the "well-dressed public" to admire its splendors as well—a bit of vanity that ended in a stampede that left some would-be visitors seriously injured and others dead.

At the Pavilion, too, George was obsessed with presenting himself as "The First Gentleman of Europe," a sobriquet he had earned in his youth due to his alleged drawing room graces. In fact, he was neither a charming companion nor a gracious host, despite the frequent balls and banquets for which he was famous; as one guest noted, "If he is caught alone, nothing can equal the execrations of the people who recognize him...All agree that [he] will die or go mad. He is worn out with fuss, fatigue and rage." He was happy only when he was the center of attention; his idea of a delightful evening was singing for hours before an audience of weary but helpless guests.

Given his obsession with securing the admiration of others, it should come as no surprise that George was also notoriously thin-skinned. After the critic Leigh Hunt described the prince as a "fat Adonis of fifty," George had him imprisoned for two years; likewise, he cast aside his erstwhile mentor Beau Brummell after the trendsetting dandy joked in public about the king's considerable girth. Late in his life he began sleeping through the day, not rising until evening, when he would receive his advisers in his bedgown. Even his impending death did nothing to slake the king's excessive appetites: he regularly consumed a breakfast consisting of two pigeons, three beefsteaks, most of a bottle of Mozelle, a glass of champagne, two glasses of port, and a glass of brandy.

When the end finally came, George was found to have left behind no state papers, but rather a collection of love letters, trinkets, and used handkerchiefs—the detritus of a life devoted to style over substance. The renowned English novelist William Makepeace Thackeray expressed the unspoken derision of the nation when he wrote of the dead king, "I look through all his life, and recognize but a bow and a grin."

Bertie's Bailiwick

ROYAL GARB

HEIGHT OF FASHION

HIS FAVORITE TRIKE

Although he was a far more intelligent and popular sovereign, England's King Edward VII—known popularly as Bertie—shared with George a passion for excess and a lifelong reputation as a royal style maker. Obsessed from boyhood with pursuing all manner of pleasure, Bertie became a legend in his own time for personifying his subjects' notion of a true gentleman: a man addicted to hunting, gambling, wenching, and his wardrobe. Indeed, though he ruled as king for only nine years, the Edwardian period of British history is named for Bertie in recognition of the panache with which he pursued passions and for his enduring influence on masculine tastes and styles.

For Bertie, taking his pleasure in style was a virtual necessity. On a hunting party in Egypt in 1869, he and his wife Alexandra traveled up the Nile on six gold and blue steamers towing barges filled with necessities such as seven thousand bottles of champagne and claret, four French chefs, riding horses, and a white donkey reserved for Alexandra's use alone. Although he succeeded in killing his first crocodile along the way—a female, nine feet (2.7m) long—he failed to shoot a hyena and had to console himself by killing innumerable cormorants, cranes, flamingoes, herons, and other birds.

After Bertie became too stout to do much big-game hunting, he took up baccarat, carrying his own counters engraved with the prince of Wales's feathers. Baccarat, of course, was illegal, and his devotion to the game threatened to become the stuff of scandal when he was subpoenaed by the prosecution in a lawsuit brought by a fellow gambler who had been accused of cheating at cards. Although Queen Victoria worried about "the light which has been thrown on his habits which alarms and shocks people so much, for the example is so bad," many ordinary Britons were unconcerned, and regarded the incident as just one more proof of Bertie's admirable cool under fire.

But it was his sense of fashion that vaulted Bertie into the ranks of legendary royal style makers. According to one biographer, he selected his clothing with great care and discussed at length with his tailor the precise styling of his waistcoats and tailcoats. His preferences were generally conservative—he tried, for example, to revive the custom of wearing knee breeches instead of trousers on formal occasions, and refused to wear a Panama hat, which he considered too formal—but he was a fashion innovator as well. His adoption of the loose, waist-banded Norfolk jacket made the style so popular in England that every gentleman still considers it indispensable; likewise, the omnipresent tuxedo owes its popularity to Bertie's habit of wearing a short, dark blue jacket with silk facings, white shirt, bow-tie, and black trousers. His other enduring contributions to men's fashion include the homburg and Tyrolean hats, the double-breasted coat, and a tradition of leaving undone the bottom button of the waistcoat—an innovation that owes its inspiration to Bertie's ever-expanding waistline.

Among the duchess of Windsor's most prized possessions were her Cartier "Great Cat" jewels.

Windsor Knots and Diamond Leopards

Some fifteen years after Bertie's death in 1910, his namesake King Edward VIII— better known as the duke of Windsor— began displaying a similar passion for excess, and became obsessed with presenting himself as an unparalleled style maker. The guiding light of the "Bright Young Things" who came of age during the Roaring Twenties, Windsor exemplified the ethos of the time, which valued style over substance.

He was famous around the world for wearing white waistcoats with tailcoats for formal occasions, a practice that was emulated by Hollywood's leading men and other would-be swells throughout the 1930s. His preference for sports clothes— bright argyle-knit golfing sweaters, casual pullovers, sporting suits in a loud check known as "Prince of Wales"—helped popularize informal attire even among those who couldn't afford to play golf or tennis. But perhaps his most enduring fashion innovation was the unusual "Windsor" knot he made in his lustrous silk ties, a practice still maintained by men around the world.

The duchess of Windsor shared her husband's passion for excess, and eventually became a style maker herself; deprived by her husband's family of the title and status she coveted, she became famous instead as one of the world's best-dressed women. Indeed, shopping was once described as her life's work, and she often booked five or six fittings a day with the world's most famous French couturiers.

But the duchess's greatest claim to fame was the collection of jewels that her husband helped her amass. Even before they were married, Windsor had presented her with a Christmas gift of fifty thousand pounds' worth of jewelry, following up a week later with sixty thousand pounds' worth of jewels for the New Year.

Since, after
Edward's
abdication
of the
throne,
they could not
direct British
politics,
the duke and
duchess of Windsor
devoted
themselves to
exercising
their influence in
the world of
style.

Part of an international social scene, Wallis and David hobnob with Maryland ex-senator Millard Tydings and Mrs. B.H. Griswold, a friend of the duchess, at a charity ball in Baltimore.

Among the most famous pieces in her vast collection was a brooch depicting a leopard paved in diamonds and sapphires, lounging on a bright blue globe— mindlessly beautiful and casually predatory, like the duchess herself. Not surprisingly, even her death was a triumph of style over substance: "I went to look at the flowers at the funeral," recalled Laura, duchess of Marlborough. "It was tragic. They were all from dressmakers, jewellers, Dior, Van Cleef, Alexandre. Those people were her life."

The death of the Windsors signalled the death knell for the lifestyle they represented so well; indeed, for the past thirty years monarchs around the world have done everything in their power—short of giving up their thrones, of course—to present themselves as models of probity and modesty. In a world no longer in thrall to their whims, nor enthralled by their majesty, the world's rulers have learned to keep their passions for excess in check, at least in public. Today, the Windsors' niece Elizabeth II, queen of England, even pays her own taxes, and has opened Buckingham Palace to tourists to help pay for the restoration of Windsor Castle, which was partially destroyed by fire in 1992. Who among her predecessors and relations, in any kingdom on earth, would have dreamed of raising money from the public to renovate a royal residence? And when else in history would a monarch have echoed Elizabeth's credo, "It is possible to have too much of a good thing"?

Twentieth-Century Chic

Unlike most of her predecessors, the royal family's most famous style maker of the nineties is a woman of substance who devotes her considerable energies to supporting a wide variety of charitable causes, from the arts to AIDS research. But despite her image as a devoted ambassador to the world outside Buckingham Palace, Diana, princess of Wales, is celebrated for being the most striking style maker to grace the royal family since the late nineteenth century. At that time, another princess of Wales, Alexandra, inspired so much adulation that even her stuttering gait, the unfortunate result of a serious illness, was widely emulated by her future subjects.

Diana's singular status as a fashion icon remains undiminished despite her separation from her husband in 1992 and retirement from public life one year later. Indeed, she is often credited with having revived singlehandedly the once-moribund British fashion industry—and not just because she always made a point of patronizing British designers. Her reputation rests just as strongly on her lavish expenditures in support of her passion for fashion. According to one biographer, she spent an estimated $1.5 million on her wardrobe during the first twelve years of her marriage—a figure that does not include her expenditures on clothing meant for informal occasions.

Of course, any number of royals have enormous wardrobes—Diana's estranged husband Charles, for example, has been accused of spending nearly as much on his clothes as his wife. What sets Diana apart from the rest is her innate sense of fashion, and the confidence with which she wears her clothes and jewels. For public appearances, she favors rich, highly saturated colors that invariably attract attention, in smartly tailored styles intended to show off a figure that's the envy of many fashion models. The obvious pleasure she takes in hats—she reportedly has a collection of seventy-five, which are stored in special dust-free hatboxes—continues to inspire admirers around the world, just as her preference for sleekly layered short hair has made the style a classic for the past fifteen years.

It is at night, though, that Diana sparkles. Attired in shimmering silks shot through with threads of silver or gold, or lavished with bugle beads or paillettes, she resembles nothing more than a radiant princess in a fairy tale. Her glittering collection of jewels seems to have sprung from a storybook romance as well. While her trademark is the many-stranded pearl choker necklace—a style first made famous by Princess Alexandra in the late 1800s—she also favors the two diamond tiaras she received as wedding gifts and the suite of diamond-and-sapphire jewels presented to her by the crown prince of Saudi Arabia. Diana's delight in fashion is especially evident in the unconventional ways she sometimes displays her priceless treasures: knotting a long rope of pearls down her back to emphasize the plunging back of a crushed velvet gown or wearing as a headband a cabochon emerald and diamond Art Deco necklace.

Whatever fate holds in store for this stylish but embattled princess, the public's love affair with Diana—and her passion for excess—are sure to endure. And

Di's Closet

In 1993, Diana owned no fewer than eighty suits, fifty daytime dresses, and more than one hundred evening gowns—all with matching accessories; all were said to have been maintained by two full-time dressers who organized her ensembles weeks in advance and kept detailed records of what the princess wore on every royal outing.

for as long as there are royals, people around the world will prefer to view them as they once viewed themselves: as exalted beings obsessed with excess and determined to pursue their every passion. The truth is, we don't want to see them any other way, for we still need to believe in the fantasies they personify.

When Irish Eyes
❧ — Are Smiling — ❧

The Kennedys

John F. and Jacqueline Bouvier Kennedy cut the cake *(left)*; the Joseph Kennedy family *(above)*.

**M**ore than two hundred years ago, Americans died by the thousands to ensure their independence from the British crown. ⚜ Today, millions of Americans are as obsessed with royalty as any loyal Briton—so much so, that fifty years ago a "royal" family in the United States ascended to a throne of sorts. Their name, of course, is Kennedy, and no other clan in America has ever come close to matching, much less surpassing, their enduring claim on the collective imagination. ⚜

As wealthy and powerful as many genuine royal families, the Kennedys are also every bit as ruthless in fulfilling their desires, ruled by their obsession with winning and their passion for sex and excess. ⚜ What's more, like so many royals, their rousing triumphs have always been leavened by heartrending tragedies—a family history that has left them singularly suited to reign in our fantasies as fairy-tale figures who mirror our deepest wishes and most pressing fears. ⚜

The First Couple

ROSE AND JOE GET MARRIED

THE MISTRESS

Gloria Swanson was only one of Joseph Kennedy's many conquests.

The first Kennedy to fascinate the American public was Joseph Patrick Kennedy, the son of an Irish immigrant who ran a tavern in Boston when he wasn't running for public office. Like the founders of virtually every royal dynasty, Joe was ruled from childhood by an overwhelming desire to force others to submit to his will; his motto, even then, was "If you can't be captain, don't play." His pugnacity was no doubt reinforced by the prejudice against Irish Catholics so prevalent in New England in the early 1900s. In fact, it seems that Joe went to Harvard precisely because he knew he would be regarded as an "untouchable"; he couldn't resist the challenge of mastering the social intricacies of that bastion of Yankee snobbery. After graduation, Joe continued to defy his blue-blooded skeptics by becoming the nation's youngest bank president at the age of twenty-five; ten years later, he was one of America's youngest millionaires as well, thanks to savvy stock market investments and, many believe, a booming business as a bootlegger. Soon he was a movie mogul and real estate magnate as well, capping off his career with stints as the chairman of the Securities and Exchange Commission and U.S. ambassador to Great Britain. The only thing he seemed to enjoy more than his money and power was ensuring that his sons would triumph over their rivals as well—a goal he achieved by launching their entry into politics and ensuring that they received only flattering coverage in the media.

In private, however, it seems that Joe was ruled by his passion for sex outside marriage—despite having fathered four sons and five daughters with his wife, the former Rose Fitzgerald, whom he married in 1914. Indeed, he appears to have led two lives: one as the enormously wealthy and powerful patriarch of the Kennedy clan, and the other as the enormously wealthy and powerful sugar daddy of a stable of beautiful mistresses.

His most famous mistress was screen siren Gloria Swanson, whom he wooed privately in Hollywood, and in front of his wife and children in Hyannis Port and Europe. He is believed to have lavished his attentions on countless other women as well, on frequent business trips across the country, and in the suites he maintained for years at the Ritz-Carlton Hotel in Boston and the Waldorf-Astoria in New York City. Even as an old man, Joe's libido remained so strong that his son Jack would warn attractive female house-guests to lock their doors before they went to bed, as his father had "a tendency to prowl late at night."

Not surprisingly, Rose shared some of the personality traits that made Joe a legend—most notably his passion for besting his rivals. But unlike Joe, Rose by most accounts was a cold, distant disciplinarian, concerned primarily with maintaining the public perception of the Kennedys as an ideal family. Thus, she pointedly ignored her husband's womanizing and focused not on nurturing her children's individual strengths, but rather on instilling in them the importance of winning at all costs. Biographers say that when her brood returned from boarding school for vacation, they were forced to compete in some kind of activity virtually every minute of the day—a "regimen that abhorred weakness and tolerated no slackers." Later, at dinner, they were expected to report formally on these pursuits, and to answer questions about their schoolwork or current affairs; then they would retire to whichever rooms they had been assigned for that vacation, having no permanent rooms of their own.

Joe, Jr. *(right)* dominated his brothers, particularly Jack, with whom he was closely competitive.

Their Firstborn

Like most children, the second generation of Kennedys inherited their parents' ruling passions. For example, their oldest sons, Joe, Jr., and Jack, derived their greatest pleasure as young men from trying to outperform each other. Typically it was Joe, Jr., who won their encounters on the playing field and in social situations; brash, self-confident, and a natural leader, he had no difficulty eclipsing Jack, who was born with an unstable back and suffered throughout his youth from a wide variety of painful, even disabling ailments. Their rivalry intensified after both enlisted for service in World War II despite their father's widely publicized and universally derided calls for Nazi appeasement.

Much to Joe, Jr.'s, chagrin, it was Jack who shipped out for combat duty first, taking command of a patrol boat in the Pacific in April 1943. Four months later, PT-109, with Jack at the helm, was cut in half by a Japanese destroyer; three of his crew were killed instantly, and two others were injured. Despite his physical frailty, Jack saved the survivors single-handedly—towing one injured man to a nearby island by means of a rope he clenched in his teeth—and then carved an SOS onto the shell of a coconut, sending it with two islanders to find help. Even though it was most likely his incompetence as a commander that had precipitated the crisis, Jack was hailed as a hero, thanks in large measure to the positive publicity his father engineered; he utimately received the Purple Heart and the Navy and Marine Corps Medals.

Soon thereafter Joe, Jr., a pilot, finally shipped out to England, where he began patrolling the Atlantic in search of German submarines. After yet another favorable article about his brother was published, Joe reportedly began gambling heavily and volunteering for extra duty. In August 1944, an apparently jealous Joe volunteered for a highly experimental and top-secret mission to pilot a bomber packed with explosives that would be guided to its target via remote control. He was killed instantly, in an explosion so devastating that it damaged several planes flying nearby.

Joe *volunteered* for a **highly** experimental and **top-secret** mission to pilot a bomber packed with **explosives.**

A Rebellious Daughter

Four years later, tragedy struck the Kennedys again, when the outspoken and vivacious Kathleen Kennedy was also killed. Reportedly Joe's favorite, Kathleen was also ruled by her passions, even when they collided headlong with the expectations of her parents. She had already confounded them by marrying Billy Cavendish, the marquess of Hartington, a Protestant English nobleman who was killed shortly thereafter by a German sniper. Then, in 1948, she fell in love with Lord Peter Fitzwilliam, a descendant of William the Conqueror and the owner of the largest private home in Europe, with 365 bedrooms. He was also a ladies' man, like her father; indeed, he was still married to another woman at the time he and Kathleen fell in love. Enraged, Rose reportedly threatened to disown her rebellious daughter rather than accept a Protestant into the family. But before she could make good on her threat, Kathleen was killed with Peter in a plane crash over France, where she had hoped to introduce him to her father. A heartbroken Joe attended the funeral, but Rose did not join him.

William Cavendish and Kathleen Kennedy smile happily at their wedding in London in 1944. Their happiness was to be short-lived, as Billy was killed only months later.

Crown Prince of the Kennedy Clan

THE WIFE

THE MOVIE STAR

THE MOB GIRL

With the deaths of his brother and sister, Jack had become his father's heir apparent—a role that enabled him to indulge even more fully in the passion for winning and extramarital sex that also ruled his father's life. Having run successfully for seats in the House of Representatives and the Senate, he, too, had developed a taste for mastering his rivals; and with his political success, he also had become a legendary womanizer.

By the time Jack met Jacqueline Bouvier, a gorgeous Catholic heiress working as an inquiring photographer for the *Washington Times-Herald,* he had allegedly enjoyed affairs with scores of beautiful women, including Inga Arvad, a twice-married Danish bombshell suspected of being a German spy during World War II. According to Kennedy biographers Peter Collier and David Horowitz, Jack's compulsive couplings were "a game of numbers, and he scored with impressive frequency...[stewardesses and secretaries] appeared almost nightly at the Georgetown house, in such numbers that Jack often didn't bother to learn their names."

Some biographers of Jack and Jackie Kennedy believe that it was just this quality in Jack that attracted Jackie—despite the pain his infidelities would bring her. Her father, "Black Jack" Bouvier, had also been a rake, and after his divorce from her mother, he is said to have treated Jackie more like a mistress than a daughter—lavishing time and presents on her when it suited him, and otherwise ignoring her

altogether. Lem Billings, Jack's best friend at the time of their engagement, told biographers that he tried to warn Jackie about Jack's predilection for adultery, but concluded that she wasn't sexually attracted to a man unless he was dangerous, like her father. The couple was married in Newport on September 12, 1953, at an elaborate ceremony that attracted more than three thousand spectators and generated the kind of fawning press coverage all the Kennedys coveted.

Marriage apparently did little to temper Jack's penchant for promiscuous sex; indeed, it is believed that he even maintained an apartment on the Potomac specifically for his assignations. Like his father, Jack was especially attracted to actresses; and just as his father had won the heart of the most beautiful actress of his day, Jack is believed to have carried on a torrid affair with the greatest sex symbol of his age, Marilyn Monroe.

According to numerous biographers, Jack first met Marilyn at a dinner party in 1954, but did not begin dating her until several years later. Even after he was elected to the presidency, he reportedly saw the voluptuous star regularly—even, by some accounts, traveling with her on Air Force One, with Marilyn disguised in a brown wig and sunglasses. According to gossip columnist Earl Wilson, Monroe was completely infatuated with Jack, and believed that her sexual prowess helped ease his chronic back pain. Their last tryst reportedly occurred in May 1962—

Jack and Jackie, king and queen of a new Camelot, ride through the streets of Washington, D.C., in an open-car parade.

just two days before a Madison Square Garden fund-raiser and birthday party for the president, where she sang a breathless version of "Happy Birthday" attired in a sequined gown so tight it literally had to be sewn on.

But Marilyn was not the only woman who slept with Jack during his presidency. Among the many one-night stands whom the Secret Service was said to have ushered in and out of the White House were at least two women who reportedly became long-term mistresses. One was Mary Pinchot Meyer, a sister-in-law of *Washington Post* editor Ben Bradlee, who supposedly introduced Jack to marijuana; she was murdered in 1964. The other was Judith Exner, a well-known Las Vegas party girl who was also the mistress of Sam Giancana, a Chicago Mafia capo who is alleged to have rigged votes

for Jack's presidential bid in Illinois and West Virginia. Exner claimed in a 1991 interview that Jack not only knew of her liaison with Giancana, but used her as a conduit to the Mafia for large sums of money as well as intelligence data about a White House plot to assassinate the Cuban leader Fidel Castro.

Why Jack, arguably the most powerful man in the world, would have jeopardized both his career and national security to satisfy his passion for sex remains a mystery, but there are some biographers who believe that he courted danger so assiduously because of a longstanding preoccupation with death.

It began, they say, in 1947, when he was diagnosed with Addison's disease, a malfunction of the adrenal glands that essentially destroys the body's immune system. At the time, the prognosis for sur-

vival was quite poor; luckily, his physicians were able to treat him with a new drug, DOCA, which had such a salutary effect that his family reportedly stashed it in safe deposit boxes all over the country, in case of emergency. By 1961, say biographers, he had become dependent on amphetamines and steroids, which were administered regularly by Dr. Max Jacobson, known to his patients as "Dr. Feelgood." Yet despite these treatments, Jack remained convinced that he was doomed to die young, and often told friends that "the point is that you've got to live every day like it's your last on earth. That's what I'm doing." What else he might have achieved by dint of this all-or-nothing approach to life will never be known; he was mowed down by an assassin's bullets on November 22, 1963, when he was only forty-six years old.

America's Princess

Jacqueline Kennedy, continually in the spotlight as First Lady, commanded headlines throughout her life, though she preferred to maintain a low profile.

After her husband was fatally shot on November 22, 1963, Jacqueline Bouvier Kennedy refused to leave the trauma room at Parkland Memorial Hospital. "How can I see anything worse than I've already seen?" she demanded of the doctors and Secret Service agents who had gathered there. Nonetheless they kept trying to shepherd her out, unaware that the First Lady was still cradling in her right hand a sizeable chunk of Jack Kennedy's brain. After she had handed it over to a doctor and the president was declared officially dead, Jackie kissed her husband's lifeless foot, then his leg, and then his thigh and chest, before kissing his lips. She never said a word, but later, when it was suggested that she change out of her blood-and-gore splattered suit, she refused in no uncertain terms: "I want them to see," she insisted, "what they have done."

Jackie's poise in the face of her husband's gruesome assassination and emotionally wrenching funeral has become the stuff of legend, but she was not always perceived as a remarkably courageous woman. Indeed, in 1963 most Americans admired Jackie less for her character than for her status as America's foremost trendsetter. The first president's wife in modern history to set fashion, she transformed forever the public's notion of what a female public figure ought to look like.

Eschewing the fussy, dowdy styles associated with other First Ladies, Jackie championed a spare, youthful elegance that proved irresistible: her simple couture dresses, bouffant hairdo, and shapely pillbox hats were copied by millions of women around the world. When she and her husband visited France, she created such a sensation that the president began joking, "I am the man who accompanied Jacqueline Kennedy to Paris." And when his political enemies accused her of spending $100,000 on her wardrobe, she had the wit to reply, "I couldn't spend that much unless I wore sable underwear."

But Jackie wasn't content simply to dress herself elegantly and bask in her fame as a fashion icon; she wanted to make a more lasting contribution to American culture. Soon after entering the White House—which, she complained to veteran journalist Hugh Sidey, reminded her of a hotel, with people standing around wherever she happened to glance—she conceived the notion of recapturing the elegance of the White House as it had been in the days of Jefferson and Madison. She began by scrounging around the White House basement for appropriate desks, tables, and chairs, and scouting out the original woodcuts for wallpapers used in the nineteenth century. In addition to overseeing every aspect of the redecoration, she devoted hours to persuading collectors to donate their treasures to the mansion, and when at last all the pieces were in place, some 80,000,000 Americans were transfixed as she graciously conducted the first televised tour of the White House in history.

That Jackie was fascinated by architectural design and preservation came as little surprise to most of the audience that evening: after all, before she moved in to the White House she had lived in a succession of lavishly appointed mansions, and had been educated at elite schools like Vassar and the Sorbonne. What was surprising was her continual defiance of the world's expectations after she left the White House, beginning with her marriage to Greek shipping tycoon Aristotle Onassis; how, they asked, could she tarnish her husband's memory, and her own place in America's royal family, by marrying such a coarse, unattractive old man? After his death left her a widow for the second time, she defied convention again by choosing as her companion Maurice Tempelsman, a married Jewish financier and diamond merchant.

By the time Jackie succumbed to non-Hodgkin's lymphoma in May 1994, the world had grown accustomed to thinking of the former First Lady not just as a fashion trendsetter—though her preference for slacks and oversized sunglasses had by then influenced two generations of women—but as an uncommonly self-possessed role model. Where once she had been admired for exchanging witty repartee with Charles De Gaulle, she was now famous for devotion to her children and grandchildren; where once she was disparaged as a gold-digger, she was now lauded for toiling in the relative obscurity of book publishing, where she specialized in editing books about the arts.

Buried in Arlington National Cemetery, beside her first husband and their infant son Patrick, she has finally been acknowledged as the woman she was all along: stylish, yes, but also smart and sensitive. "Her style was not vanity," declared Richard Martin, associate curator of the Metropolitan Museum of Art in New York, whose collections include couture clothing donated by Jackie anonymously. In fact, he said, her style was "a way of living, not simply adorning herself but expressing her vision of beauty in the world." And that is how she will no doubt be remembered.

What was *surprising* was her continual defiance of the world's expectations after she left the White House.

Jackie walks with Maurice Tempelsman in New York City's Central Park shortly before her death from non-Hodgkin's lymphoma.

Whispers of Scandal

Jack achieved greater prominence than any other member of the second generation of Kennedys, but he wasn't the only member of the family who inherited Joe's competitive drive and passion for sex. For example, some family biographers believe that Jack's younger brother Bobby—the straight arrow of the family, and the father of eleven children—carried on an extramarital affair with Marilyn Monroe that was much more serious than the president's. It began, they say, when Jack dispatched Bobby to California to break off his relationship with the sex goddess— and he and she unexpectedly fell for each other. Some believe that Marilyn was convinced that Bobby would divorce his wife Ethel and marry her, and that she took a

Marilyn Monroe and Peter Lawford.

fatal overdose of barbiturates in August 1962, after he ended their affair.

Bobby denied being in Los Angeles on the day that Marilyn died; however, his brother-in-law Peter Lawford, the "Rat Pack" actor who initially introduced Marilyn and Jack, reportedly admitted years later that Bobby had indeed gone to her house. It has been widely speculated that Lawford went there as well, after she took the overdose, in order to destroy any evidence he could find linking her and the Kennedys. Like Marilyn, and his siblings Joe, Jr., Kathleen, and Jack, Bobby also died tragically, after being shot by an assassin while celebrating his victory in the California presidential primary in June 1968.

Bobby poses with his wife Ethel Skakel Kennedy, their ten children, and the family dog; an eleventh child was born after Bobby's death.

A somber Ted and Joan Kennedy leave Hyannis for the funeral of Mary Jo Kopechne.

✠

The car
hurtled
thirty-five feet

through

the air,

landing

upside down.

✠

Shouts of Scandal

Teddy Kennedy, Jack's successor as U.S. senator from Massachusetts, has also been branded a womanizer by family biographers. The youngest of the Kennedys, he married one-time model Joan Bennett in 1958 and, like his father and brothers, reportedly began breaking his marriage vows almost at once. After he came close to dying in a 1964 plane crash, he allegedly began pursuing his extramarital relationships with greater ardor and less discretion. Five years later, many Kennedy colleagues and friends were not surprised to learn that he had been driving late at night with a beautiful young woman who had once campaigned for his brother Bobby. What was shocking was the role he played in Mary Jo Kopechne's death in a tidalpool off Chappaquidick Island in Massachusetts.

According to biographers, after attending a party on Chappaquidick Island that included several other young women who had worked for Bobby, Ted left with Mary Jo, presumably to take the midnight ferry back to nearby Martha's Vineyard. Unfamiliar with the roads, he made a wrong turn and, unable to turn around, continued driving until his 1967 Olds somehow

Chappaquidick in Print

The tragedy at Chappaquidick has spawned an abundance of books, all purporting to uncover the true nature of the accident. Here is a sampling of Chappaquidick theories:

Senatorial Privilege: The Chappaquidick Cover-Up, Leo Damore. The author describes how Paul Markham, a friend of Ted, and Joe Gargan, a cousin, also dove into the pond to search for Mary Jo, but found the current too strong. According to Damore, the senator hoped that it would appear to her rescuers as though the young secretary had been alone when the car plunged off the bridge.

The Bridge at Chappaquidick, Jack Olsen. In this scenario Mary Jo was, in fact, alone when the car hurtled off Dike Bridge, Ted having exited the vehicle after it was spotted by a police officer.

Teddy Bare: The Last of the Kennedy Clan, Zad Rust. The author claims that Ted jumped from his speeding car before it crashed into the pond, and then conspired with others to cover up the tragedy.

Death At Chappaquidick, Richard and Thomas Tedrow. The senator was unaware that Mary Jo had fallen asleep in the back seat of his car when he left the party for the ferry.

Chappaquidick Revealed, Kenneth Kappel. The author speculates that the senator crashed the car into some trees before reaching the bridge, injuring Mary Jo so severely that she lapsed into a coma. Then, according to Kappel, the senator and two friends pushed the car off the bridge and into the pond, with Mary Jo still inside.

struck Dike Bridge; moments later, his car had hurtled thirty-five feet (10.6m) through the air, landing upside down.

Teddy managed to escape from the submerged vehicle, and told police that he dived repeatedly back into the murky water to see if his passenger was still in the car; but when he couldn't find her, he walked back to the cottage, where the party was still in full swing. Still in a state of shock, he said, he swam back to Martha's Vineyard, failing to inform police about the accident until the next morning. Although others apparently realized that Mary Jo might still be trapped inside the senator's car, no one else called the police, either, and she was left to die, possibly by suffocation.

It was at this point, some believe, that a cover-up of the tragedy was engineered by the Kennedy family and their advisers. Within hours of the time that Mary Jo's body was found, the five other attractive campaign workers attending the party had left Chappaquidick Island, before they could be interviewed by police. Then, after the media badgered an apparently unwilling district attorney into requesting an inquest, the hearing wasn't held until six months later—after the senator was allegedly told precisely which questions he would be asked.

After his negligence was found to have been the probable cause of Mary Jo's death, Ted made an emotional speech on television, denying that excessive consumption of alcohol had played any role in the accident, as well as any improper relationship with the dead woman. Then he stunned viewers by suggesting that he might step down from office—a preemptive strike against his political opponents, who were surely

impressed by the enormous number of telephone calls and telegrams urging him to shoulder on. In typical Kennedy fashion, he had finessed the media and turned tragedy to his advantage.

Like his brother Jack, Teddy was apparently ruled so strongly by his passion for sex that he continued to have affairs throughout his marriage to Joan, which ended in divorce in 1982, two years after his unsuccessful bid for the presidency. Rumors about his womanizing and drinking became even more widespread in the years that followed, until his wedding in 1992 to attorney Victoria Reggie.

Ted's marriage to Victoria Reggie has done much to assuage his reputation for drinking and womanizing.

Peter Lawford and Patricia Kennedy cut the cake at their wedding reception at the Plaza Hotel in New York City. Like other Kennedy women, Patricia had a marriage that was marred by the infidelities of her husband.

Scandal-in-Law

But Teddy was not the only member of the Kennedy clan dedicated to excess, according to biographers. His brother-in-law Peter Lawford, the English actor who married Patricia Kennedy in 1954, was apparently also ruled by scandalous desires. According to Rose Kennedy's former private secretary, Peter was raised as a girl until the age of nine—at which point his nanny taught him to perform oral sex, presumably adding to his sexual confusion. Despite having received no other education to speak of, and an injury that nearly severed his arm, he became a movie star and one of the most visible members of the Kennedy clan.

Like his brothers-in-law, Peter apparently began his marriage by committing adultery. According to Rose's secretary, he also participated vicariously in Jack Kennedy's extramarital escapades, acting as the president's procurer and as his go-between with the mob—roles that guaranteed him a prominence that had previously eluded him in Hollywood.

Given these proclivities, it is not surprising that his relationship with Pat eventually deteriorated. Within days of her brother Jack's assassination, Pat packed up her children and moved to New York without her husband, reportedly masking her despair with alcohol and pills. After their divorce on the grounds of mental cruelty in 1966, it is believed that Peter turned increasingly to drugs and alcohol, sacrificing virtually every important relationship he had ever formed before he died of cardiac failure and cirrhosis in 1984.

The Secret

Perhaps the most heavily guarded secret maintained by the second generation of Kennedys was the mental retardation of Rosemary Kennedy, whose handicap was especially glaring in a family that valued success above all else. Born in 1918, she was treated during her childhood like the rest of her siblings, in a fruitless attempt by Rose to convince herself and others that Rosemary was just like them. As she matured, however, it became increasingly apparent that Rosemary would never be able to share fully in the social lives of her sisters; and when her father became concerned that her disability might become a political liability for his sons, she was allegedly forced to undergo a prefrontal lobotomy in 1941.

Afterward, the wild mood swings that had so troubled her family disappeared as hoped, but with them went Rosemary's personality and attachment to the family. Eventually, they decided to institutionalize her at a nursing convent, where she wouldn't be as great a burden on her family. Outsiders were told that Rosemary had "chosen to devote her life to a religious order working with retarded children." That she herself was retarded remained a secret for years.

Rose and Rosemary, dressed for their appearance at the court of King James of England.

The Third Generation

HEIRS TO THE THRONE

John, Jr., and Caroline continue the family tradition of public service at a movie premiere to benefit the Robert F. Kennedy Memorial Fund.

By the time the next generation of Kennedys entered adolescence, in the early 1970s, the family's legacy of public service and private scandal had been established. In particular, the family's longstanding passions—for winning at all costs, sexual promiscuity, and alcohol and drugs—now seemed like genetic imperatives too strong to be denied among many of these thirty young men and women. The boys in particular were ruled by these obsessions, perhaps because it was they who were expected to grow into men as powerful and successful as Jack, Bobby, and Ted. Bobby's

assassination had been an especially tragic loss for them, as it had robbed them of one of the strongest male role models they had ever known within the clan. Say photographers Peter Collier and David Horowitz, "he was the one who had defined their Kennedyness, and now that he was dead, the definitions were all called into question."

Among those who questioned their identity most persistently were two of Bobby's older sons, Bobby, Jr., and David, as well as two of his nephews, Bobby Shriver and Christopher Lawford. Beginning in the summer of 1968, they

allegedly began experimenting with a wide array of drugs; all were eventually arrested for drug possession. Bobby Kennedy, Jr., and Chris developed addictions so severe that they were forced to undergo treatment, but at least their rehabilitation was successful; David, on the other hand, was never able to overcome his problem, and he died of a drug overdose in Palm Beach during the Easter holiday of 1984.

Spending Easter at Palm Beach was also a mistake for another member of the third generation of Kennedys: William Kennedy Smith, who was charged in

1991 with raping a twenty-nine-year-old Florida woman on the beach outside the Kennedy compound there.

A son of Jean Kennedy Smith and wealthy business executive Stephen Smith—the Kennedy family "fixer" who was responsible for untangling the potentially scandalous political and personal problems of various in-laws—Willie was a thirty-year-old physician when he met his accuser at a popular local bar late on the night of Good Friday. He had gone there to drink with his uncle Ted and cousin Patrick Kennedy, who returned that night to the family estate with a guest of their own, a waitress who later claimed to have seen the senator walking through the mansion wearing nothing but an Oxford shirt.

Willie and his accuser also returned to the mansion, and then walked along the beach. Then, his accuser charged, he removed his clothing and jumped into the ocean for a nude swim; deciding it was time to leave, she said she had started walking back toward the house when Willie tackled and raped her. Willie, on the other hand, claimed that she had consented willingly to rough, unprotected sex on the beach, with his lawyers charging that she had accused him of rape because of previous unhappy sexual experiences.

In the aftermath of his arrest, charges of past sexual assaults, including rape, were recounted to the media. Ted was also savaged in the press, by allegations that he was a longstanding alcoholic and that he had participated actively in a cover-up of the incident—charges that no doubt reminded voters of similar press accounts after Mary Jo Kopechne was killed near Chappaquidick. Ultimately, Willie was acquitted, but not before his reputation had been irremediably harmed, along with the reputations of his uncle and cousin.

Though Willie remains more notorious than famous, his once-troubled cousins have achieved a great measure of professional and personal satisfaction in their lives. Bobby Kennedy, Jr., is an attorney specializing in environmental law; Chris Lawford is a television star; and Bobby Shriver is a venture capitalist and part-owner of the Baltimore Orioles.

Many of the other cousins are highly successful as well. Joseph Kennedy II is a congressman from Massachusetts; Caroline Kennedy Schlossberg is an attorney and author; John Kennedy, Jr., is an attorney who was voted *People* magazine's "Sexiest Man Alive" in 1988; Maria Shriver is a television news anchor married to superstar Arnold Schwarzenegger; Kerry Kennedy is the legal counsel to the Robert F. Kennedy Memorial Fund, a human rights activist, and wife of Andrew Cuomo, son of New York's former governor; Kathleen Kennedy is the head of the Maryland Student Service Alliance; and Michael Kennedy is the chairman of the Citizens Energy Corporation.

Still, despite their many achievements, it is the family's flaws that continue to fascinate the world. Every day, historians, biographers, journalists, screenwriters, novelists, muckrakers, and talk-show hosts scramble to uncover some new scandal surrounding the Kennedys—and given the depth of their ruling passions, a treasure trove of scandalous secrets is no doubt waiting to be discovered. But no matter what other unpleasant truths are revealed, the Kennedys will retain their hold on our collective imagination.

After being found not guilty of sexual assault and battery, William Kennedy Smith, backed by his family and supporters, addresses the press at a news conference outside the Palm Beach County Courthouse.

CHAPTER FIVE

Live

and Let Die

The murder of Thomas Becket *(left)*; The duchess of York *(above)*.

ver since the day that Cain succumbed to sibling rivalry and murdered his brother Abel in a field, feuding has been a human tradition. ⚜

And like every other tradition that has spanned civilizations since, feuding has been practiced with particular passion by the world's royal families. In fact, for most of history, feuding is what royalty have done best. ⚜ As ruthless as toddlers at protecting their possessions—and every bit as outraged when their demands have been denied—they have spent centuries trying to define themselves by defying others. ⚜ Unlike children, however, when they've met with resistance, more often than not they've resorted to warfare, preferring the potential spoils of victory to the certain humiliation of backing down from a fight. ⚜

Treachery in Egypt

Feuding among members of the same royal family has been a feature of every dynasty in history. Three thousand years ago, the first Egyptian queen, Hatshepsut, came to power after her father died and she was forced by custom to marry her frail, effeminate half-brother. A few years later, he was murdered—Egyptologists who unearthed his remains discovered that his shoulders, hips, pelvis, and breastbone had been broken—and Hatshepsut, his probable assassin, became regent for Thutmose III, her dead husband's nine-year-old son by a concubine. To consolidate her power, she married the boy to her daughter, thus becoming his mother-in-law as well as his aunt and stepmother; but after a few years of governing in Thutmose's place, she decided to simply declare herself queen and let him try, if he could, to unseat her.

To reinforce the notion that a woman was qualified to rule all of Egypt, Hatshepsut erected innumerable statues representing her as a pharaoh with a beard, and then built an enormous temple at Deir el-Bahari decorated with hieroglyphics indicating that she was a direct descendant of the venerated sun god Amon. Scenes painted and inscribed on the walls at Deir el-Bahari depicted

Hatshepsut's "divine birth" and showed Thutmose I, her father, crowning her king. These representations were intended to justify Hatshepsut's claim to the throne and to glorify her reign. As transparent as they might seem to us, these subterfuges apparently fooled the Egyptians; Hatshepsut ruled for twenty-one years, until she was murdered, presumably by her son-in-law Thutmose III.

Having been victimized by his predecessor for virtually all of his life, Thutmose wasn't content simply with replacing her on the throne; he was determined to obliterate all traces of her reign. Under his orders, the noses of all statues of Hatshepsut were hacked off and dumped into a quarry, and her face and name were removed from all state records. More confident now of his own power, Thutmose channeled his remaining energies into conquering Asia, slaughtering untold numbers of its inhabitants and bringing home to Egypt all the money and treasures his army could carry. Eventually he reigned over an empire that included Thebes, southwest Asia, and the Sudan, relying mainly on local princes to maintain his authority.

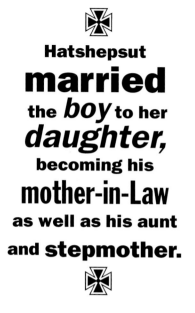

One of the surviving statues of Queen Hatshepsut from Deir el-Bahari depicts her in the full regalia of a pharaoh, including a beard.

Hatshepsut **married** the *boy* to her *daughter,* becoming his **mother-in-Law** as well as his aunt and **stepmother.**

Hatshepsut's Broken Legacy

As long ago as 3000 B.C., the Egyptians believed that as long as material images of the dead endured, their lives would continue in their tombs. For this reason, they mummified their dead and buried along with them the objects, food, treasures—even the bathrooms—needed to ensure their repose in the afterlife. Regarded as links between mortal men and the gods, the pharaohs were entombed with special attention to their comfort and spiritual needs in the afterlife.

The pharaoh Hatshepsut chose Deir el-Bahari, across the Nile from the temples of Karnak and Luxor, as the site of her mortuary temple. Although it has been only partially preserved, archaeologists believe that it was a terraced structure, partly rock-cut and partly free-standing, surrounded by trees, flowerbeds, and innumerable statues and sphinxes. A second temple, which has completely disappeared, is believed to have been even more monumental, featuring courts at three different levels as well as immense reliefs depicting, among other scenes, the divine birth and coronation of Hatshepsut. Thutmose erased all of these images of her in relief, and smashed all of the colossal statues of his nemesis, replacing them with figures of himself.

Like Mother, Like Son

Among the ancient Romans, no emperor could compete with Nero at any number of royal pursuits, not the least of them feuding. Born in A.D. 37, Nero was a son of two murderers: Cnaeus Domitius Ahenobarbus, who especially enjoyed gouging out the eyes of his victims, and Agrippina the Younger, a sister of Caligula who is believed to have murdered the two husbands she took after Cnaeus's death. One of these husbands was the Emperor Claudius, to whom she allegedly fed mushrooms laced with arsenic to ensure the accession of her son and sometimes lover, Nero.

Given his lineage, it is not surprising that Nero was also ruled by his parents' passion for murder. Described as a bisexual satyr with a swollen belly, spindly legs, tangled yellow hair, and lusterless gray eyes, he killed his first wife, a daughter of his stepfather Claudius, by smothering her in a steam bath; he murdered his second wife, Poppaea, by kicking her savagely while she was pregnant.

His mother was also one of Nero's victims. He killed her when he was only twenty-one—old enough to be annoyed by her continual interference in state affairs, but young enough to try to kill her painlessly, in acknowledgment of all he owed her. He tried a fast-acting poison, but after it failed three times to achieve its desired effect, he rigged the ceiling in her bedroom to collapse and crush her while she slept. This plot was frustrated, too, as was the next, an attempted drowning at sea. At his wits' end, Nero finally ordered one of his freedman to dispose of Agrippina as he pleased, and the former slave promptly beat her to death with a club.

Nero receives the body of his mother, Agrippina the Younger, whom he had murdered after she opposed his marriage to the ambitious and unscrupulous Poppaea Sabina.

The Generation Gap

In ancient China, royal parents and children often sought to unseat one another. In 624 China's first emperor set in motion a feud that rocked his empire when he named as his heir apparent the eldest of his three sons. Enraged, his middle son, T'ai-tsung, murdered both of his brothers and forced his father to abdicate in his favor.

Twenty-five years later, after T'ai-tsung's death, his father's erstwhile concubine followed T'ai-tsung's example by wresting the throne from his legitimate heir. The notorious Empress Wu went on to name her son as her successor, and when he rebelled against her domination, she installed her youngest son in his place. She then forced the boy to abdicate in her favor, declaring herself founder of a new dynasty, the Chou. She was finally overthrown—by her son—and the multigenerational feuding she helped inaugurate became a staple of imperial family successions.

All Gaul Is Divided...

In France, rivalry in the royal family nearly destroyed the nation's first dynasty just a few years after it was established in 458. After the death of the first French king, his son Clovis succeeded him to the throne without opposition. Soon thereafter, he married the daughter of the king of the Burgundii and converted to Catholicism, establishing the inextricable link between the French monarchy and the Vatican. A ruthless adversary, Clovis managed to defeat nearly all his rivals in battle—including some members of his wife's family—and died in 511 after having consolidated under his rule the territories that now constitute France.

Clovis spent his life uniting the Franks, mostly by assassinating or conquering rival Frankish kings, and by the end of his reign he had extended the territory of his kingdom from northern France to the Mediterranean.

This rendering of the education of the children of Clovis, painted by Lawrence Alma-Tadema, shows the emphasis on military skills that, in the end, served them perhaps too well.

Brunhilda, a Visigothic princess before her marriage to Sigebert, influenced two generations of Frankish kings before her brutal execution by Clotaire II in 613.

Unfortunately, the battles that preoccupied Clovis's four sons—Theodoric, Clodomir, Childebert, and Clotaire—were fought mostly among themselves, as each coveted the land his father had left the other. A pact for mutual support foundered with the death of Clodomir, and for the next forty-seven years, his brothers and their children tried to assassinate one another. The nation wasn't reunified until Clotaire, the only surviving party to the original vendetta, managed to take the throne and rule without opposition for three years.

Clotaire's death in 561 provoked a new round of feuding among his four sons, who shared the family passion for mastery and revenge. When they weren't engaged in combat on the battlefield, they spent their time hatching plots aimed at assassinating other members of the family.

But the deadliest members of this fourth generation of French royals were not the sons but their wives. The most infamous was Fredegund, who married one of Clotaire's sons after strangling her predecessor in her bed. Afterward, she killed both her brother-in-law and her stepson and tried to kill a second brother-in-law and a nephew.

Fredegund's sister-in-law Brunhilda was almost as notorious. After Fredegund murdered Brunhilda's husband, Brunhilda apparently decided to take family matters into her own hands. First she tried to marry her nephew; next, she ordered the assassination of her great-nephew; then she deposed the sons of another great-nephew so that she could install her great-grandson on the throne. She was finally neutralized by her nephew Clotaire II, who tortured her for three days before tying her by an arm and a leg to the tail of a wild horse, which trampled her to death.

Brother Against Brother

Feuds among English royalty have been rife as well, with many having been kindled by sibling rivalries that persisted for generations. One of the most far-reaching of these multigenerational vendettas was set in motion in 1087, when William the Conqueror divided his kingdom by leaving the duchy of Normandy in France to his eldest son, Robert; the throne of England to his middle son, William Rufus; and five thousand pounds to his youngest son, Henry.

Like royal siblings everywhere, the brothers immediately conspired against one another, with William and Robert joining forces to prevent Henry from ever claiming their dominions. But when King William Rufus was killed in 1100—having been shot with an arrow in the New Forest, allegedly at Henry's command—it was not Duke Robert who ascended the throne, but rather his murderous little brother. As expected, Robert immediately invaded England seeking the crown, but Henry eventually defeated him in the battle of Tinchebrai—and then kept him prisoner for the next twenty-eight years, to ensure his continued humiliation.

The feud among William's children did not end with Henry's victory, however, for despite holding the record for fathering more illegitimate children than any other English monarch, he had only one surviving legitimate heir—his arrogant

Stephen's wife petitions Empress Matilda for her husband's release. An exchange for Matilda's brother, who was being held by Stephen's forces, was eventually arranged.

Family Feud

Feuds between kings and queens have also been commonplace in England. Perhaps the most scandalous involved Henry's descendant Edward II, a crude, cowardly monarch who was toppled from his throne by a queen eager to capitalize on his passion for other men. Even before he was crowned in 1307, Edward II had enraged his family by his homosexual attachment to Piers Gaveston, a Gascon knight. According to a contemporary chronicler, Edward's persistent efforts to enhance his lover's power and wealth finally led his father to attack him, shouting, "'As the Lord lives, if it were not for fear of breaking up the kingdom you should never enjoy your inheritance.' And seizing a tuft of the prince's hair in each hand, he tore out as much as he could, until he was exhausted, when he threw him out."

But despite his family's violent objections, Edward's reliance on his lover became even more pronounced, culminating in his appointment of Gaveston as regent in 1308—the same year the king was wed to the twelve-year-old Isabella of France. As Gaveston's influence at court continued to grow, the barons became increasingly resentful of the king's lover, and three years later they ambushed and murdered him. But neither Gaveston's death, nor the birth of his first child, prevented Edward from establishing a new, and even kinkier, homosexual relationship with two new favorites, Hugh Despenser and his father.

Humiliated, Isabella began feuding with her husband as well, returning in disgust to the court of her brother, King Charles IV of France, in 1325. There, she took as

daughter Matilda—and he was determined that she should succeed him in place of his nephews. Nonetheless, at Henry's death the barons renounced their support of Matilda and crowned her cousin Stephen of Blois in her place.

His coronation in 1135 provoked a feud far more deadly than the one pursued by his uncles. Reputed to be the most handsome, best-natured man in England, Stephen was more popular with the rabble than Matilda; but when her husband, uncle, and half-brother all rallied their considerable forces behind her, Stephen was unable to raise an army large enough to defeat them. The ensuing civil war lasted for years, with each cousin maintaining a separate royal court, and each enduring temporary imprisonment at the hands of the other. Finally, after untold numbers had perished, Stephen agreed to accept Matilda's son as his heir, and was crowned on Christmas Day in 1141. After Stephen's death, Henry II began his thirty-five-year reign over an empire stretching from Ireland to the Pyrenees.

But King Henry II soon revealed that he shared his ancestors' passion for feuding. His most infamous feud was with his one-time friend and chancellor, Thomas Becket. After having been appointed archbishop of Canterbury, Becket underwent a religious conversion that ended in a jealous dispute about the king's customary rights over the Church; and when Henry complained that his servants "let their lord be treated with such shameful contempt by a low-born clerk," four of his knights killed Becket in Canterbury Cathedral.

In fact, Henry's deadliest enemies were his own four sons, who had grown up conspiring with their mother to usurp his throne. The most dangerous of them, the future kings John and Richard I, were so envious of their father's power that they joined forces against him with King Philip II of France—who apparently enjoyed Richard as a lover as well as an ally. Henry died just two days after his ignominious defeat at their hands, leaving behind him on a wall in Winchester Castle a horrifying epitaph: a mural featuring four eaglets in the process of dismembering their helpless parents.

Queen Isabella began intriguing against her husband, Edward II, almost as soon as they were married. Her quarrels with Hugh Despenser, a favorite of the king, led to the seizing of her properties, a severe cut in her allowance, and surveillance of her activities, though this did not prevent her from overthrowing the king.

his genitals were cut off and dispersed. Afterward, his head was chopped off and sent to London, while his body was hacked into quarters and dispatched to four other cities.

Edward's death at the hands of his queen and her lover was even more barbaric. According to a historian of his reign, the king was initially imprisoned in Berkeley Castle, "where he was tortured for many days....There with cushions heavier than fifteen strong men could carry, they held him down suffocating him. Then they thrust a plumber's soldering iron, heated red hot, guided by a tube inserted into his bowels, and thus they burnt his innards and vital organs." Two months later, he was buried in Gloucester Abbey, but without his heart—Isabella reportedly had it removed and placed it in a silver case, for eventual burial in her own coffin.

A Holy War

But perhaps the strangest feud in British royal history involved two sovereigns who never even met: Queen Elizabeth I of England and Mary, Queen of Scots. For twenty-seven years the greatest fear of each was that she would be unseated by the other, an anxiety that not only reflected the ongoing strife between Protestants and Catholics in sixteenth-century Britain, but one that eventually changed forever the face of the empire.

Their feud began in 1533 with the birth of Elizabeth to King Henry VIII and Anne Boleyn. Four years later, Anne was executed on trumped-up charges of adultery, and Elizabeth became persona non grata at court, hateful to her father because she reminded him of Anne, and hateful to her

her lover the exiled baron Roger Mortimer, and began plotting the overthrow of her husband—when she wasn't busy trying to destroy the marriages of her three brothers, by accusing their wives of adultery. When Edward ordered her to return, Isabella—the only known adulteress among medieval English queens—replied, "I feel that marriage is a joining together of man and woman...and that someone has come between my husband and myself trying to break this bond; I protest that I will not return until this intruder is removed, but, discarding

my marriage garment, shall assume the robes of widowhood and mourning until I am avenged of this Pharisee."

Nonetheless, the following year Isabella returned to England with Mortimer and her son. The trio was greeted enthusiastically by a populace eager to see her husband deposed; the queen, on the other hand, wanted to see him dead. She quickly ordered the capture of her husband's lover, Sir Hugh Despenser, who was then led on a forced march to Hereford, where he was tied to a ladder and set on fire; simultaneously, father's opponents because they perceived her as a Protestant bastard. A precocious child who had inherited her father's intellect and her mother's vitality, she responded to her newly diminished status by asking her governess, "how hap it yesterday Lady Princess, and today but Lady Elizabeth?"

Elizabeth's Catholic cousin Mary Stuart was born in Scotland to king James V in 1542 and, like Elizabeth, was thrust from birth into a maelstrom of religious politics. After Henry VIII was denied the infant princess as a bride for his son and heir, he invaded Scotland. To fend off further English aggression, Mary was betrothed at the age of six to the Catholic heir to the throne of France, and sent to live there.

Ten years later, Mary's cousin and namesake, Queen Mary of England, died, and the Scottish princess was declared heir to the throne by her fellow Catholics. Nonetheless, it was the Protestant Elizabeth who was crowned in England on January 15, 1559, while Mary became the queen of France. Mary's reign was cut short, however, by the death of her sickly young husband, and she returned to Scotland to ascend the throne there—having never renounced her claim to the throne of England.

Frightened by this challenge to her sovereignty, Elizabeth escalated the hostilities by financing an abortive coup after Mary married Lord Darnley—a cousin of both who had a claim to Elizabeth's throne—and bore him a son. How much of a role Elizabeth played in Mary's subsequent downfall is still a mystery, but one thing is certain: she was delighted when Mary was forced to abdicate, and lost no time in imprisoning the Scottish queen after she fled from her homeland to England.

Mary remained Elizabeth's captive for nineteen years, serving as a beacon of hope for England's disgruntled Catholics, who were determined to return a coreligionist to the throne. Elizabeth was worried by their fervor, but she refused to move against her cousin until she was formally petitioned by Parliament to authorize Mary's execution to prevent a Catholic rebellion. Even then, she equivocated, replying, "If I should say unto you that I mean not to grant your petition, by my faith I should say unto you more than perhaps I mean. And if I should say unto you that I mean to grant your petition, I should then tell you more than is fit for you to know."

Nonetheless, Mary was beheaded at Fotheringay Castle on February 8, 1587, dressed for the occasion in a red petticoat, red satin bodice, and a wig—which flew off as soon as the executioner held up her severed head. When he went to remove her other adornments, he found a tiny Skye terrier shaking uncontrollably beneath her skirts. The dead queen's heart and other organs were buried deep beneath the castle grounds.

Hearing the news of her death, Elizabeth broke into copious tears, and wrote to Mary's son in Scotland that his mother's death had been "a miserable accident." No one can say for sure whether Elizabeth had somehow convinced herself that this was true, or whether she was simply reluctant to own up to murder among her other sins. In any case, Mary's death and the end of their feud came as a great relief—so great, in fact, that Elizabeth named Mary's son James as her heir, paving the way for a new British empire comprising England, Ireland, and Scotland.

Mary dressed for her beheading in a *red* petticoat, red *satin bodice,* and a wig.

Elizabeth signs Mary's death warrant; though Mary's execution was politically expedient, it took a severe emotional toll on Elizabeth.

Political Plots and Philandering

Ippolito quickly avenged the *insult* by ordering his grooms to *stab* Giulio in both eyes.

Renaissance Italy was also a hotbed of internecine strife, and here, too, the exigencies of geography helped inflame jealous feuds among royalty: with dominions too diminutive to be divided, relatives who were denied succession often sought retribution through bloody coups.

When Ercole d'Este was installed as Duke of Ferrara in 1471, his nephew Niccolo immediately began plotting a coup against him. After his first attempt failed, he tried again, only to be captured and beheaded by his uncle—who nevertheless insisted on mounting a lavish funeral for the dead rebel. During the ceremony, the mourners were amazed to discover that Niccolo's body had been arrayed by Ercole in a magnificent robe of gold brocade, and his head carefully sewn back on, topped with a crimson cap. It seemed that their feud had ended at last—that is, until Ercole ordered the execution of five hundred of Niccolo's supporters, waiting until after his nephew had been buried so as not to diminish the dignity of the occasion.

But the Este clan feuded about more than political power; sex was also a primary concern, especially among Ercole's numerous male offspring. Perhaps the most famous case of sibling rivalry to rock the dynasty was inspired by the love of two of his sons for the same woman. Angela Borgia was a beautiful teenager

Alfonso d'Este survived the plots arranged by his brothers, who paid a high price for their disloyalty.

when she first came to Ferrara as a lady-in-waiting to her cousin Lucrezia, who had married Ercole's son and heir, Alfonso. It wasn't long before she attracted the notice of Alfonso's brother Cardinal Ippolito, and his half-brother Giulio, who is believed to have fathered her illegitimate child. Not content to simply rebuff Ippolito's unwanted advances, Angela taunted him by declaring that Giulio's eyes were more precious to her than Ippolito's entire body—an insult that Ippolito quickly avenged by ordering his grooms to stab Giulio in both eyes.

Torn between justice and expediency—a rare problem for an Este, since expediency was almost always the preferred alternative—Alfonso tried to reconcile his brothers before their feud caused even more mayhem; but the maimed Giulio was bent on revenge, and soon enlisted the aid of another brother, Ferrante, in a conspiracy aimed at both Ippolito and Alfonso. Their plan was discovered, however, and Alfonso ordered his two rebellious brothers to watch the beheading and quartering of their combined forces. In a measure that would disarm his brothers permanently, he condemned them both to imprisonment in his castle, where Ferrante died forty-three years later, ten years before Giulio finally regained his freedom.

All in the Family

In czarist Russia too, sex fueled feuds within the imperial family; one such vendetta, which pitted Catherine the Great against her husband, Czar Peter III, changed the course of history.

It began with Peter's impotence and Catherine's unquenchable desire for sex, and exploded into open warfare with Peter's accession to the throne in 1762. The couple had never been anything but alienated from each other, but when Peter publicly lambasted Catherine during a diplomatic banquet, her many supporters within the army felt compelled to retaliate. Two months later, her lover, Grigory Orlov, masterminded a palace coup in which Catherine was proclaimed czarina in the Cathedral of Kazan, while Peter prepared to celebrate his name day elsewhere. After demanding his immediate abdication in her favor, Catherine ordered Peter's imprisonment; less than two weeks later, he was dead, and less than two months after his murder, his widow was crowned Catherine II in a ceremony of unparalleled splendor.

While Catherine's coronation delighted the vast majority of Russians, they soon regretted their support for her coup, as she proved to be one of the most repressive rulers in czarist history. But it was her son, Czar Paul I, who avenged her murderous plotting—albeit after her death in 1796. He had his father's body exhumed from its ignoble burial place, and reburied beside that of the czarina, forcing his father's mortal enemy, Catherine's erstwhile lover Orlov, to lead the funeral march. But Paul administered the coup de grace to his mother's memory when he also exhumed the body of her most cherished lover,

Potemkin—and insisted that the corpse remain above ground, so that it could be devoured by birds.

Catherine's Coronation

Given the fact that she came to power through the assassination of her husband, it is not surprising that Catherine spared no expense when it came to declaring herself empress of all Russia. Recognizing immediately the importance of looking like a legitimate ruler, she invested a small fortune in her coronation, which was far more opulent than the ceremonies enjoyed by any of her predecessors.

Her robes were breathtaking, fashioned from 4,000 ermine skins, but the pièce de résistance was her crown. Representing the pinnacle of eighteenth-century jewelry-making, it was decorated with 5,012 diamonds, seventy-six enormous oriental pearls, a diamond cross, and a 425-carat spinel ruby. The solid gold orb she carried was garlanded with a band of diamonds and a forty-seven-carat sapphire, while the famous 193-carat Orlov diamond, the fourth-largest in the world, graced her sceptre.

In the Land of the Rising Sun

In eighteenth-century Japan, the emperor was considered a sacred ruler with direct links to the spirits that inhabit the land. So removed from politics was the imperial family that it had ceded nearly all its power to a handful of distantly related princes known as samurai. Family members were forbidden to leave their walled compound without express permission. Lest their isolation inspire insurrection, they were ordered to spend all their time doing what they enjoyed most—studying—while the shoguns who actually ruled Japan engaged in bloody feuds with one another.

By the nineteenth and twentieth centuries, royalty around the world had experienced the same diminution of political power as their peers in Japan; and while many continued to be ruled by their passion for feuding, their vendettas no longer ended in murder. In the new climate of egalitarianism, royals were too busy trying to save their monarchies from extinction to devote much time to killing off one another. As it became increasingly clear that their royal prerogatives depended on their capacity to command the public's imagination rather than their obedience, royalty became increasingly adept at presenting their families as idealized versions of our own—and at hiding any feuds that threatened to rock their empires.

Nonetheless, some feuds have been too bitter even for royalty to conceal. One of the saddest and strangest is the feud that has pitted Empress Michiko of Japan against the Imperial Household Agency, the twentieth-century equivalent of the shogunate that ran the lives of the imperial family for centuries. The feuding apparently began when Emperor Akihito married Michiko, the first commoner to enter the imperial family, against the wishes of his mother and the agency. It is believed by many that their constant criticism of the new empress contributed significantly to the nervous breakdown she suffered early in her marriage, and to a tragic miscarriage.

It remains to be seen whether the newest member of the royal family, Princess Masako, shown here with her husband, the crown prince Naruhito, will endure the same hostility showered on Empress Michiko by the Imperial Household Agency.

After their son, Crown Prince Naruhito, followed in his father's footsteps by announcing his engagement to a commoner, the Imperial Household Agency objected strongly again; but like his father, Naruhito married his betrothed nonetheless, in June 1993. Apparently stung by this second defeat, the Household Agency began leaking stories to the media purporting to reveal Michiko's true character as a domineering, extravagant, and insensitive woman unworthy of her exalted station—causing Michiko to suffer severe depression, as well as a minor stroke, which left her unable to speak for seven months. Interestingly, the Japanese people forced the media to recant their stories about Michiko, with some groups going so far as to try to assassinate two of the offending magazine publishers.

In-Law Trouble

The public response in Britain to reports of royal family feuds has been quite different from that in Japan: there, scandal sells better than romance at the newsstand. After years of trying desperately to keep their disagreements from becoming public, it seems that British royalty have embraced the media as partners in their vendettas, ruled more by their passion for mastery and revenge than discretion or even common sense.

One of the most notable royal family feuds played out through the media in recent years was occasioned by the marriage in 1977 of Queen Elizabeth's cousin, Prince Michael of Kent, to the former Baroness Christine von Reibnitz, a beautiful Austrian Catholic aristocrat. According to a Windsor biographer, Michael first met Christine when she was still married to a British banker and mourning the tragic death of her alleged lover, Prince William of Gloucester—coincidentally, Michael's cousin and best friend. Drawn together in sorrow, Michael and Christine apparently fell in love, and asked the Windsor paterfamilias, Lord Mountbatten, for his help in preventing a scandal. What concerned them most was the archaic British laws that forbid anyone in the line of royal succession from marrying a Catholic.

Influenced, no doubt, by Mountbatten's support for the couple and by her own longstanding affection for her cousin, Queen Elizabeth reportedly agreed to permit the marriage, but only on three conditions: that Michael renounce his claim to the throne; that he and his wife agree to raise their children as Anglicans; and that Christine convert to the Anglican faith.

When Christine refused to comply with this last condition, the couple was wed in a civil ceremony in Vienna, with Christine—who had been given the title Princess Michael—in a fury over the debate about her religion and suitability for membership in the royal family.

But her feud with her in-laws did not commence in earnest until after her honeymoon, when the new princess paid a visit to the long-exiled duchess of Windsor, Wallis Simpson, who was still blamed by the royal family for the abdication of her husband, the former Edward VIII. Outraged by Princess Michael's defiant support for the duchess, the Windsors apparently sought revenge through the media; according to Windsor biographer Peter Fearon, "unkind gossip items about the princess and her relationship with the queen began to appear—judicious leaks by palace officials....The palace let Fleet Street know that it was open season on Princess Michael." Indeed, it is believed that reporters were actively encouraged to investigate the seemingly mysterious background of the princess's father, Baron Gunther von Reibnitz—even though, says a royal family chronicler, "it is inconceivable that the queen and other members of the royal family were unaware of [his] shocking past" when it was ultimately revealed by the *London Daily Mirror* in 1985.

That shocking past included the baron's former membership in the Nazi party and his participation in the SS; and while there was no evidence that he was party to any wartime atrocities, the idea that his daughter had married a British

Outraged by Princess Michael's *defiant* support for the duchess, the Windsors apparently sought **revenge** through the *media.*

Prince and Princess Michael of Kent.

prince was anathema to many Britons. Ironically, of course, the queen's own in-laws, Philip's family, were linked to the Nazi party, and when the media frenzy began to threaten them as well, Buckingham Palace apparently backed off—though allegedly not before helping to circulate rumors that Princess Michael was involved with an American oilman.

Despite efforts to destroy her reputation and her marriage, Princess Michael has recouped both, thanks in part to the media's participation in the Windsors' latest obsession: their apparent vendetta against Fergie, the volatile, outspoken duchess of York, whose clashes with the royal family began almost from her introduction.

Fergie vs. Buckingham Palace

The redheaded daughter of Major Ronald Ferguson, one of Britain's best polo players, Fergie was christened Sarah, and grew up practically next door to Windsor Castle. In many ways, her childhood resembled that of her future sister-in-law, Diana: both became acquainted with the royal family as children; both were left to be raised by their fathers after their mothers fell in love with millionaires; and both were educated rather poorly. Given their affinities, it is not surprising that Diana thought of introducing Fergie to Charles's brother Prince Andrew in 1985.

Then a helicopter pilot on active duty in the Royal Navy, "Randy Andy" had nevertheless found the time to date a succession of attractive young women, including Koo Stark, an American actress best known for her roles in pornographic movies. Although Fergie was obviously a more suitable companion than a porno queen, his mother is said to have been suspicious from the start of Fergie's interest in her second-born son.

Andrew, however, was smitten, and he proposed to Fergie, despite his mother's reservations, in February 1986. Five months later, the couple was married at Westminster Abbey in a ceremony notable for Fergie's ostentatious and

unflattering gown, and for her continual mugging during a subsequent appearance with Andrew on the balcony of Buckingham Palace.

While Fergie initially charmed the public with her informality and sense of fun, her utter lack of propriety—and her relentless pursuit of publicity and perks—soon began to trouble ordinary British citizens as well as their sovereign. By 1989, the duchess's indifference to her husband and infant daughter, Beatrice, had become apparent, and she had begun spending more and more time traveling outside England without them. Among her new companions was the Texas millionaire Steve Wyatt.

According to Windsor biographer Peter Fearon, the queen was deeply disturbed by the prospect of scandal, and ordered her daughter-in-law to stop seeing Wyatt; when Fergie refused, "a plot was hatched to discredit the errant duchess. Mysterious men with military bearing had already begun laying the groundwork, holding clandestine meetings with newspaper reporters and offering information on the duchess that only insiders would know." In late 1991, 120 photographs of Fergie and Wyatt, taken secretly while they vacationed together

Fergie's lavish vacations and public appearances with men other than her husband were indiscretions neither the palace nor the press would ignore. Here, Fergie is escorted by financial advisor John Bryan.

Prince Andrew's dalliances before his marriage included one with porno star Koo Stark, whom Queen Elizabeth, not surprisingly, considered inappropriate as a daughter-in-law.

in Morocco, were brought to Wyatt's recently vacated London apartment and "left there deliberately by British intelligence agents so they might find their way to the newspapers."

Two weeks later, the London tabloids were filled with stories about Fergie's relationship with a man other than her husband. Unbelievably, however, Fergie didn't recognize the tacit warning she had received; for even while lawyers were secretly negotiating her separation from Andrew, she is believed to have been arranging a vacation with John Bryan, a friend of Wyatt's who was supposedly her financial adviser. On March 19, 1992, Buckingham Palace announced that Fergie and Andrew had separated; in a private, off-the-record briefing held later for

reporters, the queen's press secretary added that "the knives are out for Fergie at the palace."

Nevertheless, it appears that Andrew was still willing to consider a reconciliation. He and his wife celebrated their sixth anniversary together, and he arranged for her to join him at Balmoral for the family's traditional August vacation. But his family, it seems, was still not satisfied with the revenge they had wreaked on Fergie. On August 19, 1992, when she joined them for breakfast, she was handed a copy of *The London Daily Mirror*. In its pages was a series of photographs showing Fergie sunbathing topless, apparently in front of her daughters, while John Bryan sucked her toes and kissed her.

According to a royal biographer, the photos had been taken secretly by professional photographers while Fergie and Bryan were on vacation, and then leaked to the media by British intelligence—at the behest of the Buckingham Palace. According to Peter Feron, "The purpose was to discredit Fergie, destroy any hope of a reconciliation, and eliminate any negotiating power she had with the royal family. After publication of the photographs she would count herself lucky to keep custody of the children."

Since then, Fergie has counted herself lucky to keep custody of anything of value in her life. Reviled around the world for her deficiencies as a parent and a wife, and slandered at home as a plagiarizer and a cheapskate, she has become a symbol of everything rotten at

the heart of contemporary culture. But whatever her failings, real or perceived, Fergie is living proof that royalty today are ruled as much as any of their ancestors by their passion for mastery and revenge.

Fergie's exuberance has translated into embarrassment for the palace more than once. In April 1994 another set of topless photos surfaced, touching off yet more controversy over the duchess's behavior.

Map of the Road back to Brunswick

ay 24th 1796 by H Humphrey New Bond St

These Boots
are Made for Walking

❦— **Royal** —❦

Divorce

Princess Caroline discovers George with Mrs. Fitzherbert *(left)*; the trial of Catherine of Aragon *(above)*.

"The only solid and lasting peace between a man and his wife is doubtless a separation," said Lord Chesterfield, whose seventeenth-century prescription for domestic tranquillity remains potent today. ⚜ Unlike the husband and wife described by Lord Chesterfield, royal spouses on the outs have rarely been content to lead separate lives. ⚜ In ancient times, male monarchs preferred either to abandon their wives or neutralize their influence by taking other wives as well—that is, when they didn't opt for banishing or murdering them. Polygamy was not an option for royal wives, but quite a few were adept at assassination. ⚜

As religion began to dominate daily life, royal divorce ignited firestorms of protest since it was widely prohibited by both church and state. Especially in the twentieth century, as divorce rates have skyrocketed among their subjects, royals wishing to divorce, or to marry divorced men or women, have found their desires threatening to rock their empires. ⚜

To Divorce or Not to Divorce

When Charlemagne had no more use for a Lombard alliance he divorced Desiderata, his Lombard wife. His immoral behavior scandalized even his barbarian subjects.

Before the Church and the aristocracy were strong enough to question royal prerogatives, monarchs who were unhappily wed were the absolute masters of their mates. In ancient Greece, when Pericles tired of his wife, Telesippe, he not only divorced her, but arranged for her to marry her third husband. Charlemagne, who became king of the Franks some twelve hundred years later in 768, solved his marital difficulties through polygamy.

He had four or five wives—though never more than two at a time—as well as several concubines. Among them, he fathered eight legitimate and ten illegitimate children, a prodigious accomplishment given that he spent most of his forty-three-year-long reign engaged in fifty-four battles.

Several hundred years later, with Catholicism firmly entrenched, French kings were prohibited from either divorc-ing their wives or taking more than one at a time. Thus, when Blanche, the wife of King Charles IV, was accused of adultery, her husband chose to end their union by annulling their marriage and sending her to a convent to live out the rest of her life. Blanche, however, was considered lucky; her sister-in-law Margaret, also accused of adultery, died in prison after her husband, the future King Louis X, had their marriage annulled.

Two Isabellas

England's King John, who succeeded his uncle Richard I in 1199, was less mindful of the Church's teachings about the sanctity of marriage. Having secured his reign by ordering the murder of his nephew Arthur, the rightful heir to the throne, John had few qualms about ending his unhappy marriage to Isabella of Gloucester. The richest heiress in England, Isabella was both barren and promiscuous, described by a contemporary chronicler as an "incestuous and depraved woman, so notoriously guilty of adultery that the king had given orders that her lovers were to be seized and throttled on her bed." After ten years of marriage, John divorced her the same year he was crowned.

The king was also a prodigious philanderer—he fathered seven or eight bastards, and lusted even after the wives of his barons—and when he became infatuated with the twelve-year-old Isabella of Angouleme, he summarily abducted and married her. After an enraged king of France retaliated by seizing John's French possessions, the English monarch immediately invaded France, quickly capturing and imprisoning Isabella's erstwhile

John's **widow** *married* her **daughter's** betrothed, Hugh, the son of her former **fiancé.**

John's divorce and his remarriage to the child-fiancée of another was extremely impolitic, and did nothing to increase his popularity with either the aristocracy or the commonfolk.

fiancé, Hugh of Lusignan, but eventually losing Normandy to superior French forces. Fifteen years later, John made an abortive effort to regain Normandy, and in the shame of defeat signed the Magna Carta in 1215 at the behest of his restive barons. He later died of dysentery after gorging himself on fruit and cider, and his widow married her daughter's betrothed, Hugh, the son of her former fiancé.

The Prophesy of the Patriarch

Some three hundred years later in Russia, Grand Prince Vasily divorced his first wife and sent her to a nunnery because she was unable to bear him an heir. Outraged, because divorce was not permitted by the Russian Church solely on the grounds of infertility, the patriarch of Jerusalem cursed the grand prince, foretelling the birth of an evil son and an empire drenched in blood. Shortly thereafter, the Prince's second wife, a Lithuanian princess, gave birth to Ivan the Terrible, proving the patriarch's prophetic powers.

Henry VIII's Unlucky Wives

England in the 1500s was also bedeviled by its monarch's desire to divorce and his ensuing conflicts with the Church. When Henry VIII ascended the throne, he was described by a visiting Italian diplomat as "the handsomest potentate I ever set eyes on; above the usual height, with an extremely fine calf to his leg, his complexion very fair and bright, with auburn hair combed straight and short...and a round face so very beautiful." Having been kept under strict supervision until his coronation in 1509, Henry was also unusually well educated: he could converse in French, Latin, and Italian; played the lute and harpischord with grace; and could best any man in the kingdom at archery and jousting. He was passionately fond of sweets as well, and particularly enjoyed delicacies like roast bustard, barbecued porpoise, and quince preserves.

Henry's most famous passions were ensuring his succession through a male heir and marrying the beauties with whom he hoped to produce a son. His first wife was Catherine of Aragon, who had been widowed by the death of Henry's brother Arthur. While she shared her new husband's interest in learning, she was shocked by the wild hilarity of the banquets, tournaments, and pageants that he adored.

By the time Henry fell in love with the more compatible Anne Boleyn, Catherine had presented him with only one surviving child, the future Queen Mary. Desperate for both a different heir and a different wife, the king ordered Cardinal Thomas Wolsey to secure him an annulment from the pope. When the pope

Henry's wives were not spared from his ruthless and bloodthirsty impulses, and only one of the six managed to remain married to him.

refused, Henry declared himself the head of the Church of England, severing his kingdom's ties with Rome and inaugurating decades of deadly religious strife.

Henry married Anne after an adulterous courtship based on genuine love; in one of his surviving letters, he wrote to her, "No more to you at this present time mine own darling for lack of time but that I would you were in my arms or I in yours for I think it long since I kissed you." Younger, prettier, wittier, and livelier than Henry's first wife, Anne was famous for her black satin nightgowns lined with black taffeta—an exceedingly unusual fashion during a time in which nearly everyone still slept nude. Yet despite his deep attraction, Henry was unfaithful to his beloved Anne as well; while wooing

her, he also seduced her sister Mary and had an illegitimate son by one of her ladies-in-waiting.

After his divorce from Catherine and marriage to Anne, the king insisted that the Church of England approve his actions; and when old friends like his chancellor, Thomas More, and the bishop of Rochester refused to sanction either his divorce or his marriage, Henry ordered their execution. But before long, Anne, too, had invoked his wrath, having also produced only a single female child, the future Queen Elizabeth I; and on May 19, 1536, Henry ordered her beheaded before all the nobility of the realm. The next day he was married again, secretly, to Jane Seymour, who had been a lady-in-waiting to both of her predecessors. In

October 1537, she became the first of Henry's wives to deliver a son, the future king Edward VI, and died just two days later, having never been crowned.

Henry was also divorced from his fourth wife, Anne of Cleves, whose charms he found to have been exaggerated immoderately by the artist charged with painting the portrait that inspired his proposal. Thomas Cromwell, who had helped arrange the marriage, was beheaded nineteen days after their divorce. His fifth wife, Catherine Howard, was also beheaded, for committing adultery. Henry's sixth and last wife, Catherine Parr, was the only one of the lot whom he didn't divorce or execute. By the time of that marriage he was grotesquely fat—so much so that instead of walking he was moved from place to place with the aid of machinery—and had been suffering for years from the debilitating effects of untreated venereal disease. Henry died on January 27, 1547; two weeks later, his coffin burst open and "all the pavement of the church was with the fat and the corrupt and putrefied blood foully imbued." What remained of his corpse was buried alongside the remains of Jane Seymour in Windsor Castle.

JANE SEYMOUR #3

ANNE OF CLEVES #4

#5 CATHERINE HOWARD

#6 CATHERINE PARR

#1 CATHERINE OF ARAGON

#2 ANNE BOLEYN

Peter's Revenge

By the time Peter the Great was crowned czar some 120 years later, divorce was a rarity among English royalty, and no longer practiced by the imperial family of Russia. Nonetheless, having traveled extensively in the relatively liberal kingdoms of Europe, Peter had become an active advocate of more relaxed relations among his unmarried subjects. He ordered women as well as men to dress in more revealing Western-style clothes and shoes, urged them to mingle freely at social functions, and decreed that arranged marriages would no longer be tolerated.

Having been forced at seventeen to marry a woman he didn't love, Peter also set about to loosen the constrictions of his own private life. First, he forced his wife to enter a convent, the equivalent in those days of a divorce; then, he secretly married an orphan servant girl from Latvia, after the birth of several of their twelve children. Four or five years later, Peter and his new wife, now known as Empress Catherine, were married again in a public ceremony, attended by two of their surviving daughters. Yet despite his own relaxed morals, Peter was as outraged as any old-fashioned Russian husband when his wife presumed to follow his lead: having discovered that Catherine had taken a lover, he had the man decapitated, put his head in a bottle of spirits, and left it in Catherine's window for good measure.

Much of Peter's youth was spent in western Europe, and there he drank and had affairs with western women. Unfortunately for Catherine, his liberal attitudes did not extend to his wife's unfaithfulness.

The Elephant and the Maypole

A few years later, King George I, the German cousin of his predecessor Queen Anne, ascended the British throne, establishing the House of Hanover as well as his reputation as a vengeful philanderer. While still a prince, he had married his cousin, the beautiful sixteen-year-old Princess Sophia Dorothea of Zell, in a match of convenience intended to reunite their dominions. Despite her beauty, George preferred the company of his mistresses and for twelve years neglected his wife shamefully—until he learned from her ladies-in-waiting that she had begun to enjoy a flirtation with Count Konigsmark. Then he flew into action: the count unaccountably disappeared, and Sophia Dorothea was banished for life to Ahlden, divorce having been ruled out as an option. Her imprisonment there paved the way for George to bring with him to England his two beloved German mistresses: the obese Mme. Kilmansegge, known as "The Elephant," and the gaunt Mme. Schulenberg, known as "The Maypole."

Toward the end of Sophia Dorothea's life, George offered to free and reinstate his long-suffering wife, who reportedly refused with the words, "If what I am accused of is true, I am unworthy of his bed; and if it is false, he is unworthy of mine." After she died in November 1726, George left her body unburied for six months in Hanover, until a French fortuneteller warned him that he would follow his wife to the grave if he continued to shirk his duties.

The remains of George's *wife's* **alleged lover** were later discovered in the *palace* under the floorboards of Sophia Dorothea's **dressing room.**

A highly superstitious man, George immediately set off for Germany with "The Maypole" in tow, convinced that he would die before he saw his son and daughter-in-law again. And he was right; for just as the fortuneteller predicted, he suffered a massive stroke en route to Hanover, dying in the room where he had been born. The remains of Count Konigsmark, his wife's alleged lover, were later discovered in the palace under the floorboards of Sophia Dorothea's dressing room.

George I spurned his beautiful wife for two ugly mistresses.

Married for Love, Married for Money

This 1786 engraving shows a goat bearing George & Mrs. Fitzherbert, a sample of the ridicule to which he was subjected by the British public and press.

One hundred years later, in 1820, George's descendant George IV ascended the British throne and ignited a new marital scandal. For years he had been known to the public as the "First Gentleman of Europe" and "Prince Charming" on account of his drawing room graces and charm. What was less well known was his illegal liaison with Maria Fitzherbert, a beautiful Catholic widow with whom he had fallen in love in 1784, while he was still prince regent. Like Elizabeth Woodville and Anne Boleyn, who were too refined to be royal mistresses, Fitzherbert also refused that honor. Indeed, she was so resistant that George felt obliged to gain her affections by stabbing himself, and vowing that he would recover only if she agreed to become his wife. They were married secretly the following year, despite Parliament's ban on marriage between royals and Catholics, by a clergyman who had been bribed to perform the ceremony.

But ten years later, George's spending had become so profligate that he needed a legal bride—and a considerable dowry—to settle his debts. It seems that he had become a compulsive shopper, spending twenty pounds every week on toiletries alone, and buying almost every personal article he required in huge quantities; walking sticks, for example, were purchased thirty at a time, and toothbrushes were delivered by the three dozen. Much more costly, of course, was the continual building, renovation, and decoration of his many royal residences.

Thus, in 1795 Lord Malmesbury was sent to Germany to negotiate for the hand of George's cousin, Princess Caroline, who could provide the dowry George demanded. She struck Malmesbury as an amiable young woman, albeit sadly deficient in her personal habits, and in his diary he recalled several discussions with her "on the toilette, on cleanliness, and on delicacy of speaking. On these points I endeavored, as far as was possible for a man, to inculcate the necessity of great and nice attention to every part of dress, as well as to what was hid, as to what was seen. (I knew she wore coarse petticoats, coarse shifts and thread stockings, and these never well washed, or changed often enough.)" He was concerned, with reason, about how the famously finicky prince regent would respond to a bride so slovenly and unsophisticated.

As it happened, Malmesbury was present for their brief introduction, noting in his diary that immediately after the couple embraced, George left the room, called for a brandy, and went to visit his mother. His drinking apparently continued; Caroline said later that her new husband was so

Mrs. Fitzherbert, first wife of George IV.

drunk on their wedding night that he was unable to make love until the morning—and that they never had sex again. She eventually moved back to Germany and didn't return to England until the death of her father-in-law, George III, in 1820. Her plan was to be crowned alongside her estranged husband.

But George had other plans. As he had when he married Maria Fitzherbert, George once again tried to circumvent both the Church and the law—this time, by attempting to secure from Parliament a divorce from Caroline on the grounds that she had committed adultery while living apart from him. Determined to be Queen of England, Caroline attended the debates surrounding her husband's Bill of Pains and Penalties, dozing off from time to time while the members of the House of Lords questioned her chastity.

She herself is said to have addressed the issue by claiming that the only time she ever committed adultery was when she slept with "Mrs. Fitzherbert's husband."

Despite George's insistence and the ineptitude of Caroline's lawyers, the House of Lords declined to present the bill to the House of Commons, and the king was denied his divorce. Though she tried to force her way into the ceremony, George was able to bar his wife from attending his coronation on July 19, 1821, where he distinguished himself by continually nodding and winking at his mistress of the moment. Caroline died just nineteen days later—some say of misery; others, of a broken heart—and was buried in Germany after a riotous London mob insisted that her coffin be carried through the streets of the city on its way to the port.

David and Wallis

Perhaps recognizing the futility of challenging laws prohibiting royalty to marry divorcées and Catholics, the British monarchs who followed George to the throne rarely sought to pit their ruling passions against the law—until December 1936, when King Edward VIII scandalized the empire by abdicating the throne to marry Wallis Warfield Simpson, a twice-divorced American.

Christened David and created the duke of Windsor after his abdication, England's eleven-month king was the eldest son of king George V and Queen Mary, parents so distant that they failed to see for three long years that their psychotic nanny was abusing both David and his younger brother Albert, the future king George VI. Her abuse apparently contributed to some of the problems the children developed later: both were subject to violent bursts of temper, and Albert suffered his whole life from recurring digestive problems and a persistent stammer. But even the royal offspring who were not in her charge failed to flourish as they might have: John was an epileptic who was forced to live in seclusion until his death at age fourteen; George was a dissolute bisexual who reportedly counted Noël Coward among his lovers; and Henry was an internationally famous womanizer.

Given these family dynamics, it is surprising that David managed to become one of the most admired men of his generation, famous for his sense of humor,

David, crowned as Edward VIII, made headlines around the world by giving up his throne to marry the woman he loved.

his stylish wardrobe, and his ability to connect with ordinary people whenever he met them. Less surprising is the fact that he sought the kind of nurturing he had never received at home from the older, married mistresses he kept from 1918 until 1933, when he fell in love with Wallis Simpson, an American with a taste for adultery as well as espionage.

Born out of wedlock in 1895 to a woman who ran either a boardinghouse or a bordello, Wallis thought she had finally escaped from the confines of her shabbily genteel life when she married Win Spencer, a navy pilot. Soon, however, they had separated, and, ever on the lookout for bigger and better things, she reportedly embarked on a series of casual affairs, including relationships with two ardent Fascists. At the same time, it is believed, she was recruited by U.S. naval intelligence for low-level espionage—a trade she apparently plied again several years later when she joined her estranged husband in China.

That Wallis lived in China for two years is widely acknowledged; what she did while she was there remains something of a mystery. Some Windsor family biographers claim that Wallis was an American spy who worked as a hostess in a fashionable brothel, where she learned the Asian lovemaking technique called fang yung, said to prolong sexual arousal in men. It has also been reported that she had a torrid affair with Mussolini's son-in-law that ended with an abortion that left her sterile. Whatever the truth of these tales, she returned from China determined to divorce her husband and remarry. In 1928 she married Ernest Simpson, a wealthy stockbroker, and moved to London.

Some claim that Wallis **was an American** **spy** **who worked as a** *hostess* **in a fashionable** **brothel.**

"Discretion is a *quality* which, though useful, *I have never* particularly admired."

INSTRUMENT OF ABDICATION

I, Edward the Eighth, of Great Britain, Ireland, and the British Dominions beyond the Seas, King, Emperor of India, do hereby declare My irrevocable determination to renounce the Throne for Myself and for My descendants, and My desire that effect should be given to this Instrument of Abdication immediately.

In token thereof I have hereunto set My hand this tenth day of December, nineteen hundred and thirty six, in the presence of the witnesses whose signatures are subscribed.

SIGNED AT
FORT BELVEDERE
IN THE PRESENCE
OF

Albert
Henry
George

Edward R I

She first met David in 1931, at a house party to which she had been invited by her old friend and his longtime mistress, Thelma, Lady Furness. Far from conventionally beautiful, Wallis was described by one acquaintance as so "flat and angular" she "could have been designed for a medieval playing card"; on the other hand, she was also said to be "wildly good-natured and friendly" with an expression that signaled "I know this is going to be loads of fun, don't you?" In any event, David was eventually smitten, and just before Christmas of 1933, they reportedly consummated their relationship in a bubble bath—an experience that apparently went to the head of the heir to the British throne. Later, it is alleged, Wallis indulged David's taste not just for fang yung, but for sadomasochistic sex games and infantilism.

In any event, the two were soon inseparable, with Wallis acting as David's hostess at his private residence, Fort Belvedere, and accompanying him on secret vacations. David seemed unperturbed by his parents' unwavering disapproval of his mistress and unconcerned about the constitutional crisis their relationship would provoke should they ever wish to marry. Indeed, he had become so dependent on Wallis that he sometimes wrote to her several times daily, using private code words like "WE," which stood for Wallis and Edward, the name he chose to take as king. This passage was typical: "A girl knows that not anybody or anything can separate WE—not even the stars—and that WE belong together forever. WE love each other more than life so God bless WE."

Wallis, however, did not appear to share his infatuation; it seems that part of her appeal to David was her capacity "to make ordinary mortals feel like princes and a prince feel like an ordinary mortal." Instead of fawning over him as did virtually everyone else in his circle, she returned his doglike affection with cold hauteur. Her greatest concern, it seems, was managing both her husband and her lover, as she noted in a letter to her Aunt Bessie: "[Ernest] and myself are far from being divorced...and everything will go on just the same as before, namely the three of us being the best of friends which will probably prove upsetting to the world as they would love to see my home broken up I suppose. I shall try and be clever enough to keep them both."

But she wasn't clever enough; in 1936, Ernest Simpson demanded a divorce from Wallis so that he could marry his mistress. David, who had acceded to the throne as Edward VIII in January, now felt emboldened to have Wallis accompany him on a widely publicized Mediterranean cruise and to a house party at Balmoral. When asked about the propriety of vacationing openly with his mistress, he replied, "Discretion is a quality which, though useful, I have never particularly admired." By the time of Wallis's divorce hearing in October, it seemed that everyone in Britain—with the exception of the king—was worried that their liaison would end in disaster. As a friend of Wallis's wrote, "the situation is extremely serious and the country is indignant; it does seem foolish that the monarchy, the oldest institution in the world after the papacy, should crash, as it may, over dear Wallis."

The ever-stylish duke and duchess relax with their dog on the lawn.

On November 13, 1936, amidst widespread speculation that the king intended to take Wallis as his wife, David reportedly received a note from the government asking him to send Wallis out of England; otherwise, his ministers threatened, they would resign en masse from the cabinet to protest the prospect of a twice-divorced American becoming queen. While it seemed at the time that this crisis was precipitated only by fears of his prospective marriage, some biographers now believe that it was in fact occasioned by fears that David was poised to pursue a separate peace with the Nazis—with Wallis's active assistance.

David's admiration for Hitler has been well documented. Even before he became king, he argued publicly for a British alliance with Germany, enraging his government and piquing the interest of the German Führer. Under the influence of German cousins like the duke of Saxe-Coburg Gotha, a deeply committed Nazi, David even went so far as to entertain a delegation of swastika-waving German veterans, and is reported to have remarked after the war, "It was no business of ours to interfere in Germany's internal affairs, either regarding Jews or regarding anything else." Just a few days after he took the throne, he reportedly told his cousin that he wished to meet privately with Hitler.

Wallis, too, is believed to have been a Nazi sympathizer; she socialized regularly with wealthy British supporters of the Führer as well as members of his government, including Joachim von Ribbentrop, who served as Hitler's ambassador to Great Britain before he was named foreign minister. But like her future husband, she apparently did not confine herself to sympathizing with the Nazis; some

Windsor biographers believe that Wallis helped David leak his own government's intelligence dispatches to Berlin.

Shortly after learning about their alleged treachery, the prime minister, Stanley Baldwin, is believed to have instigated a bloodless coup—not by presenting Parliament with evidence of David's spying, but by ensuring that the king would have no choice but to abdicate if he wanted to marry Wallis. The ultimatum on Wallis that the cabinet delivered to the king was the first step in this process.

David, unaware of the true nature of the conspiracy, played into his ministers' hands by announcing that "if the government opposes the marriage, then I am prepared to go." When he finally realized that no one was making a serious effort to change his mind, he tried to backpedal by proposing a morganatic marriage to Wallis, which would prevent her from taking the title of queen; but this suggestion was rejected as well, and it soon became clear that the only options available to the king were breaking his engagement to Wallis or abdicating the throne. Whenever his mother, Queen Mary, urged him to remember his duty, he replied, "All that matters is our happiness."

With David unwilling to rule his empire without Wallis by his side, Parliament passed into law a Bill of Abdication on December 10, 1936. That night, after nursing a whiskey-and-soda while enjoying a pedicure, he addressed the British people in a now legendary radio broadcast, explaining that he had "found it impossible to...discharge my duty as king...without the help and support of the woman I love." Afterward, he turned to an onlooker and remarked, "It is a far better thing I go to." As he would quickly discover, however, few others shared his vision of the future as a far better thing—not even his valet, who refused that night to remain in his service. "He gave up his job," the man later explained, "so I gave up mine."

David and Wallis finally were married in France on June 3, 1937, without any members of his family present. It was a ceremony that struck one guest as "pitiable and tragic," for while David had tears streaming down his face, his bride appeared totally unmoved: "If [Wallis] occasionally showed a glimmer of softness, took his arm, looked at him as though she loved him one would warm towards her but her attitude is so correct. The effect is of a woman unmoved by the infatuated love of a younger man. Let's hope she lets up in private with him otherwise it must be grim."

Wallis's characteristic iciness became even more pronounced after she and her new husband learned that the royal family had decided to make her a royal duchess but not a royal highness—an insult that

offended them so deeply they vowed never to return to England together.

But as it happened, the royal family didn't want them back—especially not after the newlyweds' much publicized visit to Nazi Germany in 1937, where David was reported to have given a modified Nazi salute. Later, when it became clear that the Germans might be planning to restore him to the throne in the event of victory over Great Britain, David and Wallis were summarily shipped off to the Bahamas, where he was made governor in 1940. Their self-imposed exile had become a royal ban.

Even after World War II, the royal family adamantly refused to receive Wallis, and David returned alone to the land he had once ruled only a few times before his mother's death in 1953. For the next twenty years, he and Wallis divided their time between France and the United States, with Wallis remaining persona non grata in the royal family until her husband's niece, Queen Elizabeth II,

finally received her in 1967. Five years later, David died of throat cancer and his body was shipped to England, where it lay in state in Saint George's Chapel. Hearing the Garter king of Arms recite David's numerous heraldic honors—including "one-time king Edward VIII of Great Britain, Ireland, and the British dominions beyond the seas, Emperor of India"—many of those in attendance were struck anew by just how much he had given up for the woman he loved.

To the royal family, however, David's abdication was not so much a romantic impulse as an act of selfish treachery that unnecessarily rocked the empire, threatening the very future of the monarchy. Thus twenty years later, when Princess Margaret wished to wed a man who had been divorced, the royal family reacted with the same stony disapproval—even though her prospective marriage to Group Captain Peter Townsend threatened nothing sacred except their exalted sense of themselves.

The Princess and the Pauper

One of the most attractive, and vivacious of all twentieth-century royals, Margaret was captivated by Peter Townsend when she was only fourteen years old. A highly decorated veteran of World War II—he was awarded both the Distinguished Service Order and a Distinguished Flying Cross—Peter came into Margaret's life in 1944, when he became the first royal equerry in history to have been selected from among the ranks of decorated officers rather than longtime family friends. Peter was soon regarded as a surrogate son by Margaret's father, King George VI—despite the kind of solidly middle-

Princess Margaret and Peter Townsend (to the left) at the launching of a ship in 1947.

class background and marriage that ordinarily disqualified outsiders from becoming true friends of the royal family. Indeed, the king thought so highly of his trusted aide that he stood godfather to Peter's second child, and even asked Peter his opinion of Prince Philip, the beau of his older daughter, the future Queen Elizabeth II.

As the years passed, Peter and his wife grew further apart, while Margaret began dating a succession of suitors, including the American entertainer Danny Kaye and the soon-to-be-notorious English politician John Profumo.

But by 1952, when the death of King George VI led his widow to name Peter the Comptroller of her Household, it had become clear that both Margaret and Peter had loved only each other all along. With his divorce from his wife—on the grounds of her adulterous liaison with a royal portrait painter—Peter finally felt free to confess his love to Margaret, and the two apparently decided to marry in February 1953.

At the time, they were aware of only two obstacles that could prevent them from becoming husband and wife. The first was an eighteenth-century law that required the princess to seek the sovereign's permission to marry if she was not yet twenty-five years of age. The second obstacle was the teachings of the Anglican Church, which sanctioned neither divorce nor remarriage after divorce. Nonetheless, Margaret and Peter were apparently led to believe that they would be allowed to marry in a civil ceremony as soon as she turned twenty-five in 1955.

But like her uncle David, Margaret was the victim of a conspiracy—in her case, a conspiracy apparently undertaken by both the prime minister and the royal family to ensure that a middle-class government employee would never become the consort of a British princess. According to Windsor biographers, six weeks after Margaret's twenty-fifth birthday in 1955, the prime minister—himself divorced—informed the princess that the government would not sanction her marriage to a divorced man. Moreover, he threatened to revoke her Civil List income and remove her from the line of royal succession if she married Peter despite the government's objections. When it seemed as

though the couple was prepared to marry nonetheless, the royal family reportedly upped the ante, informing Margaret that she and Peter would be expected to marry and live abroad for at least ten years. It is believed that the royal family had been angered by Margaret's willingness to eschew her place in the line of royal succession.

The thought of enduring a long exile overseas, where her husband would be unlikely to find employment and both would be hounded by the press, was apparently overwhelming; after a week of deliberation, Margaret issued a statement announcing that she had decided not to marry Peter, being "mindful of the Church's teaching that Christian marriage is indissoluble and conscious of my duty to the Commonwealth."

But according to biographer Peter Fearon the statement obscured the true reason for their breakup: the opposition of her family and the government to a man who was not of their class. "Had Townsend been of aristocratic birth and with a significant income, no great constitutional issues would have been raised to prevent the couple from marrying....The shame of having to live off his wife's family could not have been used as leverage."

Margaret did her duty to the family by marrying an appropriate man, but she later became the first member of the British royal family to divorce since Henry VIII in the sixteenth century.

Anthony Armstrong-Jones, who kept the title Lord Snowdon after his divorce from Margaret, appears with his new wife, Lucy Lindsay Hogg.

Although they continued to see each other secretly, both Margaret and Peter eventually formed new attachments; and when she learned from Peter in 1959 that he had become engaged, she decided that same night to accept a proposal of marriage from Anthony Armstrong-Jones, the wealthy Bohemian photographer she had been dating for several years. They were wed in May 1960 in a ceremony that was broadcast live on television, and those millions of Britons who had once grieved along with Margaret now rejoiced in her newfound happiness.

But living happily ever after her fairy-tale wedding seems to have been just as difficult for Margaret as giving up her first love. By 1969 she and her husband, who had been created Lord Snowdon, had decided to lead separate lives—he at his estate in the countryside and she at her retreat on the Caribbean island of Mustique. By 1974 their mutual alienation seemed complete, as newspapers report-

ed that both had fallen in love with new partners. Snowdon's new love was Lucy Lindsay Hogg, a divorced Australian documentary film producer, while Margaret was reported to be involved in a torrid romance with Roddy Llewellyn, a ne'er-do-well clerk at the College of Heralds who was some twenty years younger than she.

After photos were published of Margaret and Roddy cavorting together in Mustique, Snowdon reportedly informed both his wife and the queen that he would seek a divorce, which was granted in 1978 with a friendly settlement. By then, it is believed, Margaret was suffering from both hepatitis and gastroenteritis, and from the effects of years of heavy drinking and smoking. Nonetheless she apparently continued to see Roddy, despite the public and private ridicule their now scandalous relationship provoked—until he fell in love with a woman closer to his own age in 1980.

A Royal Turnaround

Perhaps recognizing that she could have prevented some of her sister's lifelong pain if she had permitted Margaret to marry Peter in 1955, Queen Elizabeth II reacted much more sympathetically when her daughter Anne, the princess royal, confessed in 1989 that she, too, had fallen in love with a royal equerry. What made the queen's stance so surprising to many Britons was that Anne was already married to another man, Mark Phillips, and was the mother of their two children.

The most industrious and private of Elizabeth's four children, Anne was married to Mark, a fellow Olympic

equestrian, in November 1973; dubbed "Fog" by his father-in-law, he was not popular among some of his in-laws, despite the fact that he could offer Anne exactly the kind of ordinary private life in the country she seemed so desperate to enjoy. Nonetheless, it is believed that their marriage was strained from the beginning—"both saw each other as a horse that needed to be mastered," says one biographer—and in 1984 they decided to lead separate lives. Their decision to seperate was allegedly prompted by newspaper reports linking Anne and one of her former bodyguards.

THE ROYAL LINE OF SUCCESSION

Any future children of the prince and princess of Wales, whether male or female, will follow Prince Henry in the line of succession, taking precedence over the queen's own children, thus pushing Prince Andrew and Prince Edward even further down the line.

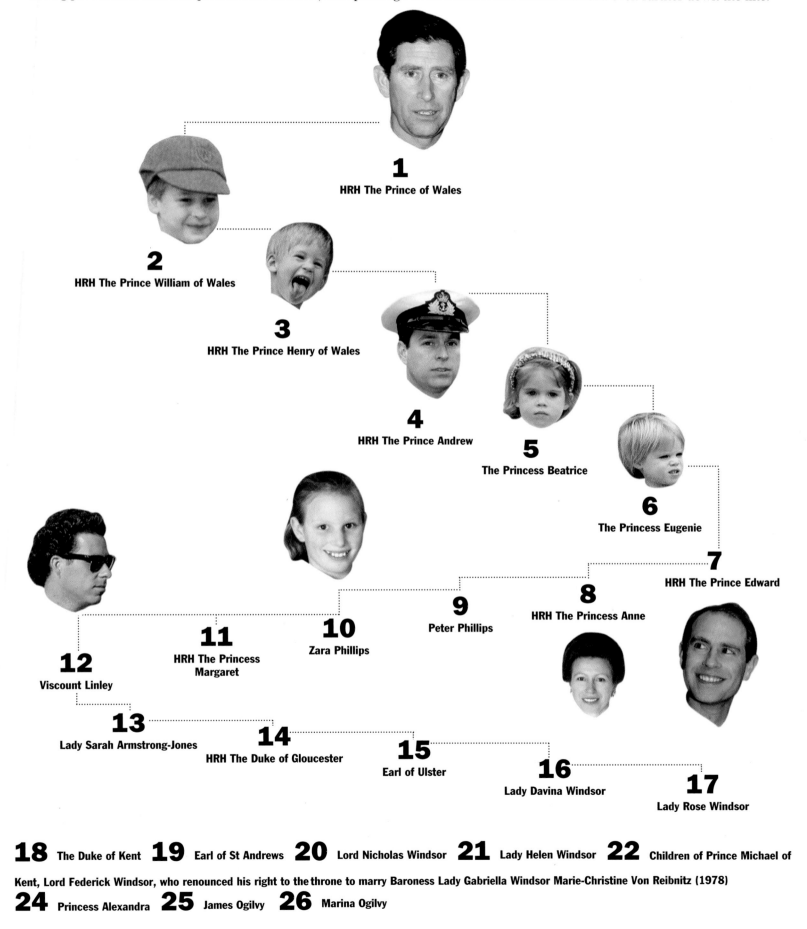

1
HRH The Prince of Wales

2
HRH The Prince William of Wales

3
HRH The Prince Henry of Wales

4
HRH The Prince Andrew

5
The Princess Beatrice

6
The Princess Eugenie

7
HRH The Prince Edward

8
HRH The Princess Anne

9
Peter Phillips

10
Zara Phillips

11
HRH The Princess Margaret

12
Viscount Linley

13
Lady Sarah Armstrong-Jones

14
HRH The Duke of Gloucester

15
Earl of Ulster

16
Lady Davina Windsor

17
Lady Rose Windsor

18 The Duke of Kent **19** Earl of St Andrews **20** Lord Nicholas Windsor **21** Lady Helen Windsor **22** Children of Prince Michael of Kent, Lord Federick Windsor, who renounced his right to the throne to marry Baroness Lady Gabriella Windsor Marie-Christine Von Reibnitz (1978) **24** Princess Alexandra **25** James Ogilvy **26** Marina Ogilvy

This new scandal involving Anne arose when love letters she had reportedly received from her mother's equerry, Commander Timothy Laurence, were stolen and sent to a London tabloid. Forty years earlier, reports of Margaret's relationship with a royal equerry had led the royal family to banish him unceremoniously to an overseas posting, without the chance to say good-bye. But unlike Group Captain Peter Townsend, Timothy was neither punished nor scorned as a mere middle-class employee unworthy of a princess. Instead, the queen insisted that he remain in her service, and even honored him with the royal Victorian Order, a personal decoration. Turning a deaf ear to the alleged objections of her mother and sons, Elizabeth broke with the traditions of the British monarchy and the Church when she sanctioned her daughter's wedding to Timothy in December 1992.

It was a small private affair at Crathie Church on the royal estate at Balmoral—a venue selected because the Church of England, which Elizabeth heads, would not recognize her daughter's union. Only a handful of royal family members attended the ceremony, among them Princess Margaret, who no doubt wondered why such a practical—albeit hypocritical—solution to her own, very similar dilemma could not have been found soon enough to suit her.

Chuck and Andy

The queen's attitude toward the tribulations of her two other married children—Prince Charles and Prince Andrew—strikes many observers as more ambivalent. On the one hand, like any mother she wants nothing more than their happiness; on the other hand, as their sovereign she cannot help but be concerned about the effects of their scandalous separations on the future of the British monarchy.

Indeed, it has been widely reported that Queen Elizabeth consulted with theologians and constitutional experts even before Charles and his wife Diana announced their separation in December 1992. Although these advisers are apparently still debating whether a divorce would prevent Charles from succeeding his mother, the *London Sun* reported that Elizabeth has already decided that she would prefer to be succeeded by Charles's eldest son, Prince William. Furthermore, newspaper accounts have alleged that the archbishop of Canterbury, George Carey, believes that Charles has disqualified himself from being king and head of the Church of England by virtue of his adulterous liaison with Camilla Parker-Bowles.

Both tradition and law make it extremely difficult for an heir to the throne to divorce, though Charles's devotion clearly lies outside his marriage.

Though Andrew and Fergie no longer live together, both make efforts to spend ample time with their young daughters. Here, Andrew and Beatrice attend Sports Day.

Whether divorce will ultimately *tear* asunder the fragile ties that still link these celebrated royals remains an open question.

Charles reportedly broke off with Camilla in late 1993, in an effort to remake his public image—an undertaking of considerable difficulty in light of his admission of adultery during a nationally televised documentary in June 1994. His confession was a public relations bonanza for his estranged wife, who announced her retirement from public life in late December 1993, reportedly in exchange for more control over the rearing of her sons William and Harry.

Prince Andrew and his wife, Fergie, the duchess of York, have also remained estranged since they began living apart in March 1992. Although Fergie undertakes no royal duties, she remains famous for her books and her volunteer work—and for being the only member of this unfortunate quartet to have acknowledged publicly that she made mistakes in her marriage. According to interviews she gave to the press on a recent American tour, she and Andrew remain on good terms and have no plans to divorce; at any rate, the duke of York sees his daughters, Beatrice and Eugenie, whenever he is on leave from commanding HMS *Cottesmore*.

Whether divorce will ultimately tear asunder the fragile ties that still link these immensely wealthy, powerful, and celebrated royals remains an open question; but whatever is decided by Charles and Diana and Andrew and Fergie, there is no doubt that the prospect of divorce has already diminished the monarchy they represent—though not their propensity for pursuing their ruling passions.

Suggested Reading

Baines, John and Jaromir, Malek. *Atlas of Ancient Egypt.* Oxford, England: Phaidon Press Ltd., 1980.

Barry, Stephen P. *Royal Secrets.* New York: Villard Books, 1985

Blundell, Nigel and Blackhall, Susan. *The Fall of the House of Windsor.* Chicago: Contemporary Books, Inc., 1992.

Boyd, Mildred. *Rules in Petticoats.* New York: Criterion Books, 1967.

Butler, Ewan. *Scandinavia.* New York: American Heritage Publishing Co., Inc., 1973.

Calloway, Stephen and Jones, Stephen. *Royal Style.* Boston: Little Brown and Company, 1991.

Cannon, John and Griffiths, Ralph. *The Oxford Illustrated History of the British Monarchy.* Oxford, England: Oxford University Press, 1988.

Collier, Peter and Horowitz, David. *The Kennedys: An American Dream.* New York: Sunmit Books, 1984.

The Complete Dog Book. New York: Howell Book House Inc.

Cuppy, Will. *The Decline and Fall of Practically Everybody.* Boston: Nonpareil Books, 1984.

Dahmer, Joseph. *Seven Medieval Kings.* New York: Doubleday & Co., Inc., 1967.

de Castries, Duc. *The Lives of the Kings and Queens of France.* New York: Alfred A. Knopf, Inc., 1979.

de Diesbach, Ghislain. *Secrets of the Gotha.* New York: Barnes & Noble Books, 1993.

Delano, Julia. *Diana, Princess of Wales.* Greenwich, Connecticut: Brompton Books Corp., 1993.

Digby, Helen. *The Royal Family Album.* Greenwich, Connecticut: Brompton Books Corp., 1993.

Donaldson, Norman and Betty. *How Did They Die?* New York: St. Martin's Press, 19

Fearon, Peter. *Buckingham Babylon: The Rise and Fall of The House of Windsor.* New York: Birch Lane Press, 1993.

Frasier, Antonia, ed. *The Lives of The Kings and Queens of England.* New York: Alfred A. Knopf, Inc., 1975.

Gibson, Barbara and Schwarz, Ted. *The Kennedys: The Third Generation.* New York: Thunder's Mouth Press, 1993.

Hibbert, Christopher. *The Emperors of China.* Chicago: Stonehenge Press Inc., 1981.

Hudson, M.E. and Clark, Mary. *Crown of a Thousand Years.* New York: Crown Publishers, Inc., 1978.

James, Ann. *The Kennedy Scandals and Tragedies.* Lincolnwood, Illinois: Publications International, Ltd., 1991.

James, Paul and Russell, Peter. *At Home with the Royal Family.* New York: Harper & Row, 1986.

Levron, Jacques. *Daily Life at Versailles in the 17th and 18th Centuries.* New York: The MacMillan Company, 1968.

Linklater, Eric. *The Royal House.* Garden City, New York: Doubleday & Company, Inc., 1970.

Lofts, Norah. *Queens of England.* New York: Doubleday & Co., Inc., 1977.

Longford, Elizabeth, ed. *The Oxford Book of Royal Anecdotes.* Oxford, England: Oxford University Press, 1991.

Macartney, C.A. *The Habsburg Empire* 1790-1918. New York: The MacMillan Company, 1969.

Massie, Robert K. and Firestone, Jeffrey. *The Last Courts of Europe.* New York: Vendome Press, 1981.

Massie, Suzanne. *Land of the Firebird.* New York: Simon & Schuster, 1982.

Morton, Andrew. *Diana Her True Story.* New York: Pocket Books, 1992.

Onassis, Jacqueline, ed. *In The Russian Style.* New York: The Viking Press, 1976.

Prescott, Orville. *Princes of the Renaissance.* New York: Random House, 1969.

Rice, Tamara Talbot. *Czars and Czarinas of Russia.* New York: Lothrop, Lee & Shepard Co., Inc., 1968.

The Royal Year 1993/94, Volume 20, Berkswell Publications Ltd., Warminster, Wiltshire, England.

Secord, William. *Dog Painting 1840-1940.* Suffolk, England: Antique Collectors' Club Ltd., 1992.

Spada, James. *Grace: The Secret Lives of a Princess.* Garden City, New York: Dolphin Books, 1987.

Wiencek, Henry. *The Lords of Japan.* Chicago: Stonehenge Press Inc., 1982.

Ziegler, Gilette. *At The Court of Versailles.* New York: E.P. Dutton and Co., Inc., 1966.

Photography credits